FIRST CHURCH OF THE NAZARENE
8801 Rogers Ave.-Route 99
Ellicott City, Maryland 21043
Phone: 1-301-465-1103

A FUTURE AND A HOPE

LLOYD OGILVIE

A FUTURE AND A HOPE

WORD PUBLISHING
Dallas · London · Sydney · Singapore

All Scripture quotations, unless otherwise noted, are from The
Holy Bible, New King James Version, copyright © 1979, 1980,
1982 by Thomas Nelson, Inc. Used by permission.

Grateful acknowledgment is made for the use of a quotation by
John Oxenham in chapter 2, from *Bees and Amber*, by permission of Desmond Dunkerley; and for quotations by John Masefield in chapter 5, reprinted with permission of the Macmillan
Publishing Company from *Poems by John Masefield* (New York:
Macmillan, 1953), and the Society of Authors (London, England)
as the literary representative of the Estate of John Masefield.

Library of Congress Cataloging-in-Publication Data

Ogilvie, Lloyd John.
    A future and a hope.

    1. Hope—Religious aspects—Christianity.
2. Ogilvie, Lloyd John.   I. Title.
BV4638.037   1988   234'.2   88-27744

ISBN 0-8499-0637-7

Printed in the United States of America

9 8 0 1 2 3 9   BKC   9 8 7 6 5 4 3

CONTENTS

ACKNOWLEDGMENTS

This is a book about authentic hope. It was written during the most difficult year of my life, a year in which I came to a deeper understanding and experience of the gift of hope.

Pascal said, "All the good maxims have been written. It only remains to put them into practice." This is especially true for the maxims of hope in the promise of God in the Bible. The book you are about to read is my own personal witness to the power of hope in physical pain, unexpected adversity, and human weakness.

Therefore, I want to acknowledge with gratitude the people who shared my journey into true hope and encouraged me in the writing of this book.

I'm deeply thankful for my family. My wife, Mary Jane, and my children, Heather, Scott, Andrew, Eileen and Jim, and my granddaughters, Erin and Airley, were a constant source of courage that spurred me on.

Special gratitude is expressed to Dr. H. J. Swan, distinguished physician, scientist, and disciple of Christ, for his wise counsel and consistent care. The healing touch, Aye!

Dr. Mark Stern, eminent orthopedic surgeon, invested his immense skills to perform a complicated surgery and put me back on my feet to walk again. I am gratified by his friendship and inspiration.

And my personal internist, Dr. Geoffrey Gean, was very helpful during my convalescence.

During this year, I have experienced in special measure the love of a congregation of hope. The First Presbyterian Church of Hollywood, my beloved congregation, graciously allowed me to discover what Paul meant when he said, "When I am weak, then I am strong."

My radio and television congregation have gloriously contradicted the false idea that the media can be only a one-way monologue. The letters and calls from across the nation expressing love and support were further evidence of the dynamic dialogue of mutual caring we share.

The completion of a book for publication is not a solo flight. It is a team effort.

The development of this book, recording what I learned in this year of new hope, was done with the enabling encouragement and the practical help of my friends and skilled editors Floyd Thatcher and Pat Wienandt. And thanks to Charles Kip Jordon, Executive Vice President, and Ernest Owen, Senior Vice President and Publisher of Word Books, who were enthusiastic prayer partners and advisers.

I am privileged to have a friend like William Mc-

Calmont, our church librarian, who does weekly research to assist me in the preparation of my sermons and my writing.

My mind is enriched by conversations with Dr. Dale Salwak and by the steady flow of classical and contemporary literature he sends me on the topic of my research at a particular time. I have appreciated his helpful suggestions for this book.

During the time of this writing, Lynda Calhoun was my Executive Secretary. Many thanks for her kindness and encouragement.

Mary Ruth Curlee typed the manuscript through several revisions. Her prayers and friendship were a special gift. Her husband, Robert Curlee, was a cheerleader and contributed his time and expertise in word processing to help us meet the deadline.

George Bayz, an Elder in our church, was of invaluable help in keeping all the computer systems on "go." I praise God for his leadership in our church and the impact of his friendship in my life.

All of these loved ones and friends have communicated authentic hope to me and made it possible to put this book into your hands so that you can claim God's promise of a future and a hope.

Lloyd John Ogilvie

Chapter One

A
FUTURE
AND
A HOPE

I might have died . . .

But God had other plans.

In what turned out to be one of the most traumatic
episodes of my life, God gave me new excitement for the
future through a dramatic experience of authentic hope.

What happened occurred after I had completed my
research for this book but hadn't actually started to
write it. The event I'm about to describe forced me to
experience personally the ideas and theories about hope
that I had been thinking about for so long.

During several weeks in the library of New College,
University of Edinburgh, Scotland, I pored over everything I could find on the subject of hope. I thoughtfully dissected every verse in the Bible in which the
word is used. Then I reflected long and hard on what
the great thinkers of all time had said and written about
hope. That process was inspiring.

But, for me, something was missing. I realized that while the word *hope* was used, it was seldom defined. The repetitive use of the word *hope* to explain hope left me frustrated and unsatisfied. It was a bit like listening to cheerleaders at a ball game. Hope, hope, hope! But the quality of hope was no more real after the cheering died down.

The essence of hope remained elusive. I was convinced that authentic hope was so much more than the shallow and glib explanations many had offered. And while the more profound works on hope were intellectually stimulating, they only brought me to the edge of experiencing authentic, lasting hope. I wanted to discover how to grow in hope and be able to communicate it to others.

⚓ Back to Old Haunts

Finally, I crammed all of my reams of notes into a bulging briefcase and headed north to a favorite haunt of mine on the rugged northwestern coastline of Scotland. Here, where the ocean winds blow out the cobwebs of the mind and where old truth becomes personal again and new insight is birthed in the soul, I could reflect and pray.

Late one Saturday afternoon while staying at a guest house near the seashore, I called my wife Mary Jane in Hollywood. We had a wonderful visit. The sound of her voice reminded me that our happy marriage was in better shape than ever. She assured me that our children and grandchildren were fine and there were no crises at the church or among our friends. We ended the long-distance visit expressing appreciation for a trouble-free period of our life and our deep love for each other. I said I'd be home in a few days.

The exhilarating conversation put me in the mood to take a long walk. It was raining, as it had been doing steadily for days, but that was no problem. I hadn't been letting that interfere with my walks. Besides that, I enjoy hiking in the Highlands in the rain. So I set out to revisit what had become a hallowed place of inspiration I'd found a couple of years before among the boulders of the rugged seashore.

Singing in the Rain

As I walked with leisurely delight, I was actually "singing in the rain." Prayers of gratitude filled my mind as I progressed down a country road, through woods, over rock fences and across the wide sheep fields. From there, I forded a shallow, rock-studded stream and picked my way down a steep and treacherous stone path to the craggy shore. It was six o'clock in the evening when I reached my destination.

Sheets of cold rain driven by strong winds beat on my face with invigorating force. Storm clouds in the sky blended with the somber drabness of the sea. Waves crashed relentlessly on majestic rock formations that nature had heaped up along the shore many centuries before.

These boulders were filled with good memories. On a previous visit, I had enjoyed climbing over them to a vantage point where I could sit alone in quiet meditation. Filled with anticipation, I headed for that spot now.

19

⚓ An Experience of Hope

Little did I know, as I prepared to spring onto the first boulder, that I was about to go through an ordeal that would change my life and radically transform my theoretical understanding of hope into an altogether new experience.

With gusto and delight, I took a running leap and began vaulting from boulder to boulder with abandonment. Perhaps a new pair of Wellington boots made me overconfident on the rocks, slickened by eight days of continuous rain, as if oil had been poured on them. As I reached the highest boulder, I remember thinking, "Lloyd, be careful." One more spring was all I needed to reach the top.

⚓ How It Happened

Then it happened. As I moved my left leg for that final leap, my right foot began to slip. I tried desperately to keep my balance. But it didn't work. Skidding and off-balance, I could feel my left leg plunging down between two boulders into a crevice so narrow it acted like a clutching vise. As I fell over to the left, all 180 pounds of me was levered on the tibia plateau of the imprisoned leg, now rigidly held between the boulders. The left side of my head and chest bashed into rocks. The blow knocked me unconscious.

I don't know how long I lay there, but piercing, throbbing pain stabbed me awake. As I regained consciousness, I realized that the upper part of my body was on one boulder, my right leg on another and my left leg was pinned between the two. I said to myself, "Lloyd, what have you done now?"

Painfully I inched up until I could sit on the boulder on the right. Then I began the excruciating process of pulling my left leg out of the rocky vise. I was alarmed to discover that not only was the pain almost unbearable but my leg felt like a limp piece of spaghetti.

When I finally had my leg freed from the crevice, I sat shivering in shock, wondering what had happened. After a time, I tried to edge myself up even further, but the leg collapsed beneath me.

Panic!

My mind raced in panic. What was I going to do? Nausea made me retch. Cold rain continued to drench me. I shivered, partly from the damp cold and partly from the physical shock my body had sustained. Alternately, I felt burning fever and cold sweat.

The grim possibilities paraded before my mind's eye as I realized what a dangerous, desolate place this was and how unlikely it would be that anyone would find me. Foolishly, I hadn't told anyone where I was going on my hiking expedition.

Probably I wouldn't even be missed until I failed to show up at dinner. Then by the time they could put together a search party, it would be pitch dark and my chances of being found before morning would be slim. I doubted I could survive the night. Even in August, the nights along the northwestern Scottish coast are damp and bitterly cold.

Then, even in the pain and haze of the moment, an ironic thought flooded my mind. Here I was, getting ready to write a book on hope, but now badly hurt and in an apparently hopeless situation.

Hope? "Yeah, Lloyd," I said to myself, "what about hope? Where's the hope you've been thinking and studying about these past weeks? The hope you've tried to tell others about all through the years?"

⚓ Help Me Out of This!

My panicked questions shifted to an urgent prayer: "Lord, I belong to you whether I live or die. But, please, help me out of this!"

As I sat shivering in pain, a desperate strategy for survival began to take shape in my mind. I knew I couldn't stand up, let alone walk. But maybe I could drag myself along on my back. By using my hands and right leg, I might be able to push myself from boulder to boulder until I reached the spot where I had begun climbing. Then I could retrace the route I'd hiked to the seaside.

I had to try! Something, Someone was pushing me. I had to move! An irresistible conviction that I could make it flooded through my mind as I was driven by a will to live!

Bolts of pain shot through my leg when I made my first move. Every bone in my body ached from the battering sustained in the fall. But slowly, after what seemed like forever, I finally edged my way off the rocks. The first lap of an arduous, seemingly impossible challenge was completed.

As I rested from the painful ordeal of pushing and sliding over the rocks, I had the haunting feeling the situation was hopeless. But each time I cried out "O

22

Lord, please help me!" a Voice responded firmly, "*We're* going to make it."

The Long Way Back

In my mind's eye, I pictured the long way back—up the steep hill, over the stone fences, across the sheep fields, through the stream, back into the forest, and finally onto the main path.

"All you have to do," the inaudible Voice kept saying, "is put your arms and hands behind you, flex up your uninjured right leg and push. Tuck your long fishing coat under your buttocks and slide. Don't think about the distance. Just make twelve pushes and then rest. Push and slide, Lloyd, push and slide!"

Following orders, I found that my heavily waxed coat did slide smoothly over the rain-soaked earth. At times as I made my way up the steep and slippery hill that descended to the sea, I would slip back a foot for every two that I made. But at least I was making some headway. After each set of twelve pushes, I'd rest and pray and call out for help.

Don't Give Up!

When I reached the top of the hill, I knew the worst was still ahead. The sheep field was level, but between it and me was a formidable high stone fence. How would I ever make it over that?

"Don't give up, Lloyd, don't give up!" the Voice encouraged me.

Bracing myself against the rocks of the fence and clawing tenaciously, rock above rock, I finally was able

23

to clutch the top of the fence. Little by little, I pulled myself up until I could put weight on my undamaged right leg. Then I fell across the top of the fence, teetering my body until I could fall down the other side. The jolt sent new flashes of pain through my entire body.

While waiting for their intensity to subside, I contemplated the ordeal of crossing the seemingly endless sheep-dung-littered field. In the backward push-and-slide motion I'd learned to use, my hands had to support my right leg. Inevitably, my hands found every gooey dung pod in the field! And it was obvious as I struggled past the sheep who were watching me that they found my grotesque crawling movements across their grazing ground both curious and frightening. It was then that even my foggy mind began to see the funny side of my desperate predicament. I had to laugh at myself. Is humor a part of hope? I think so. At least it gave me something else to think about for a while.

At the other side of the field was another fence. Same climb required. Deeper cuts in my hands. Another fall after I had finally boosted myself to the top.

Fording the shallow stream on my back left my energies even more depleted. Any part of me not drenched by the downpouring rain was now soaked to the skin. My teeth rattled as the cold seemed to penetrate every inch of my body. "You can't stop now, Lloyd. Push and slide. Through the woods. The main path is just beyond!"

By the time I made it through the woods and onto the path, I was drifting in and out of consciousness. In my lucid moments, I realized that I had pressed on to reach this point because I knew that my only possibility of being found would be by a passing walker. "Lord, send someone to help!"

After each twelve pushes and slides, I would cry out loud, "Help! I've broken my leg. Someone, please help me!" Silence. No reply. No help.

What If I Didn't Make It?

I'm not sure just when I gave in to the possibility that I might not make it. I guess it was when my voice gave out from persistent shouts for help. I had tried so hard, and it hadn't worked.

Then the question flashed through my mind—what if I didn't make it? I was not afraid of death, and in those moments I didn't make any death-road promises —no "Lord, if You get me out of this, I'll do this or that for You!" There was just a longing for the Lord Himself. But at the same time I wondered, where was He now, and why didn't He send someone to help?

Meanwhile, my mind drifted back over the past. The faces of my family, loved ones and friends came into sharp focus. I sobbed with gratitude. Then all the plans for the future flashed across my mind with vivid intensity. "Push, Lloyd, push!"

A Promise of Hope

My body screamed in protest; I couldn't move another inch. It was then, in that depleted, desperate moment, that a favorite verse in Jeremiah raced across my mind. I had memorized it years before, and now it came back to me as a personal promise. "For I know the thoughts that I think toward you, says the Lord, thoughts of peace and not of evil, to give you a future and a hope. Then you will call upon Me and go and pray to Me, and I will listen to you. And you will seek Me and find Me, when you search for Me with all your heart" (Jer. 29:11–13).

"Lloyd, I'm going to give you a future and a hope," the Lord seemed to be saying. "Trust Me. You are not finished! I don't just give hope. *I am your Hope!*" As I lay there, I thought long and hard about that amazing assurance.

⚓ A Response to Hope

In response I prayed, "Lord, forgive me. I wanted Your help more than I wanted You. You are my only hope. I surrender my survival to You."

Strangely, during my time of prayer, it had stopped raining. "That's a good sign," I thought. And it was.

About a half hour after it stopped raining, I saw in the distance three people leisurely walking along another path. My pulse beat faster as I called out to them with a raspy voice. They didn't hear me at first, and I tried desperately to shout louder. Finally they turned and walked in my direction. As they got closer, I could see that there were a middle-aged man and two teenagers, a boy and a girl.

"Please help me! I've injured my leg and can't walk," I pleaded.

"Don't worry," the man said, kneeling down beside me. "I'm a doctor. Now let me look at that leg."

Skillfully, with trained hands, he took hold of my injured left leg. When he moved it sideways, I shrieked with pain. "A nasty injury," he said sympathetically.

"Who are you? How did this happen, and how did you get here?"

I told him who I was and what had happened. I added how thankful I was that he "happened" to come along the path. "You're an answer to prayer!" I said, overwhelmed with gratitude and relief.

The doctor smiled warmly and said that he too sensed the propitious timing of his evening walk. Then he introduced himself and his children. He was a cardiologist from Edinburgh. He and his family were on holiday, staying in a nearby cottage. They had decided to take a walk that evening *when the rain had stopped!*

"Good thing we found you," he said. "You probably would not have made it through the night out here alone. It's obvious you're in extreme pain and shock. You need medical attention as soon as possible. There's a farmer down the road who has a Land Rover. We'll go fetch him and be back as quickly as we can. Then we'll get you to the local physician."

Leaving me with his son, the doctor and his daughter ran off in search of the farmer and his Land Rover.

When I checked my watch, I saw that it was 8:45 P.M. I had been dragging myself for two hours and forty-five minutes! But I had never been alone. Hope Himself had been with me every foot of the way. And the appearance of the doctor and his son and daughter on the path was just the first of a succession of serendipities the Lord of hope had planned.

Why, Lord?

As I waited for the doctor to return, questions swirled around in my mind. Why had this happened?

The Lord had not caused it, I knew. Yes, it had been foolish of me to go hiking by myself in weather like that and on rugged terrain like those boulders.

But then when I was hurt, why had the Lord waited so long to send help? Even in the fog of my pain, I somehow knew the answer to my own questions. It was when I gave up and surrendered the seemingly impossible circumstances to the Lord that I had made one of the most crucial discoveries of my life: authentic hope is born when we trust Him completely. Hope is a Person. In those two and three-fourths hours, I had come to know Him more profoundly than ever before.

⚓ Another Surprise of Grace

The next surprise of grace was meeting the local medical officer. After a long jarring ride over bumpy roads, I was carried into his home office and placed on his examining table. After I told him what had happened, he carefully slipped my battered pants off to expose my injured leg. I made an innocuous and apologetic comment, "Sorry to interrupt your Saturday evening, doctor."

"Not to worry," the Scots physician replied cheerily. "I was just preparing a children's sermon. The men in our church are taking turns, and I'm up tomorrow. I don't suppose you've ever had to give a children's sermon," he said, continuing his examination and obviously trying to take my mind off the pain.

"I've given hundreds of them over the years," I said, squirming in pain, wondering when I'd ever give another sermon of any kind.

"Ah, then, you're a dominie," he said, smiling

broadly. "I'm a Christian too! I'll be glad to tell you about that while we wait for the ambulance."

"Ambulance!" I protested. "Where are you sending me? Can't you just fix that leg here, give me some crutches and send me on my way?"

"My friend," the doctor said seriously, "it's not going to be that simple. Your leg is badly injured, and your whole body has been through an arduous ordeal. You'll have to be hospitalized in Fort William for some time before we can arrange to have you transferred back home. And after that, I suspect you have a long, difficult road ahead." My heart sank as the doctor covered me with blankets and his wife gave me their family's hot water bottle to counteract my shivering.

A phone call to the local ambulance driver informed the doctor that the area's ambulance was broken down. There was nothing to do but call for one from Fort William, two hours away by road.

This involved another painful wait. But while we were waiting, the doctor and his wife told me about their faith journey. The doctor shared the moving story of his conversion while reading a book by Joni Eareckson. "Don't suppose you know of her, do you?" he asked.

"She's a friend of mine!" I exclaimed.

With that beginning we talked for the next two hours about the Lord and we prayed together. Thinking of Joni's paralysis put my injury into perspective. The Lord had certainly used her witness in this doctor's life.

When the ambulance finally arrived, I was given a strong shot of morphine and placed on a stretcher. As

I was put in the ambulance, the doctor's wife said tenderly, patting me on the cheek, "So sorry this happened to you. We'll be praying for you. But, you should know this has been the best fellowship we've had in a long time. It's lonely up here, you know. You came a long way to bless us!"

The seriousness of my injury began to sink in as the ambulance raced through the night to Fort William. As I drifted into the numbness of medicated sleep, I kept repeating the promise I had been given by the God of hope—"I have plans for you . . . a future and a hope . . . I will be found by you . . . call on Me . . ."

⚓ The Next Morning

I awoke the next morning in a ward of the Fort William Hospital. Standing around my bed were a doctor and several interns in long white coats. They were discussing my case as they studied x-rays that had been taken in the wee hours while I was still sedated.

"A very badly crushed tibia plateau," the doctor said.

"Best thing to do is put him in a full leg cast and hope for the best," one of the interns contributed thoughtfully.

"He'll be off his feet for a long time," another said. "And we'll have to tell him he'll probably walk with a bad limp the rest of his life."

The doctor noticed I was coming out of the sedation. After questioning me about the accident, she cautioned, "You are in no shape to travel. Your body is badly battered up, and you're suffering from extreme exhaustion. You'll need to stay here for at least a week of rest. Tomorrow we'll cast your leg. Then we'll ship you home to the United States."

"How long will I be in a cast?" I asked anxiously.

"Several months," the doctor replied. "It will take a long time after that to learn to walk again. And I should warn you, you'll undoubtedly have to walk with a limp."

When the doctors left the ward, once again the icy cold hand of panic gripped my heart. What about my schedule? My work at church? A television program that could not long be sustained with reruns? One slip on a rock had not only crushed my leg but had smashed all my carefully laid plans!

A Fall in the Fast Lane

I had run in the fast lane at top speed for years. Even study times away from Hollywood were round-the-clock work periods. And brief vacations were simply to catch my breath so I could start running again. Now I couldn't even walk!

But still the Lord kept reminding me, "I have plans. My future, My hope!"

When I called Mary Jane to come help me get home, she responded with her customary resiliency. Plans for our own vacation sometime later in the month were quickly canceled, and the money was used for her round-trip journey of mercy.

The flight home wasn't easy. I didn't like being wheeled onto the airplane in a wheel chair. It was difficult to find a place to put my casted left leg during the long hours of flight. We had to change planes in Toronto, requiring us to transfer to another terminal.

They loaded me onto a crowded bus through a back door. The driver drove both fast and recklessly.

On one of the sharp turns, my wheel chair was sent rolling across the aisle, bashing my casted leg into the other side of the bus. The people on the bus shouted at the driver, "Hey, be careful! Don't you know we have a cripple on board?" The mishap not only caused more pain in my leg, it wounded my pride. I'd never been called a cripple before.

⚓ Home at Last!

Back in Los Angeles, I immediately sought the counsel of the finest orthopedic surgeon I could find. He agreed with the diagnosis of the Fort William doctors, but not the prognosis. He recommended immediate surgery.

The tibia bone and its plateau were in seven broken pieces, the knee and ligaments around it badly damaged, and the meniscus between the femur and the tibia was torn from its place. The leg would have to be rebuilt, using portions of the bone of my hip and metal screws. A few hours later, I was in the hospital. The surgery was a complicated, prolonged procedure. With great skill, my orthopedic surgeon put me back together.

⚓ The Long Process

The long process of convalescence began. During the weeks in bed, it was wonderful to know that people were thinking about me. When the pain and frustration were most intense, their cards, letters and calls of love and encouragement were a tremendous boost. Some were downright humorous.

One letter came from a man in Texas. Guess what? It was an invitation to play in a volleyball tournament to be held in Crystal Beach, Texas, ten months later! There I was, stretched out in bed, and this man wanted me to think about playing volleyball. I knew that would be too soon, but just imagining it spurred me on. I would close my eyes and picture leaping in the air, bashing the ball down over the net.

And then there was a perfectly timed call that came during one of my toughest times. "Lloyd," my friend said, "My wife and I want you and Mary Jane to go skiing with us." I laughed out loud. "Skiing? How can I do that?"

"Not this winter, Lloyd, next year!" he chuckled.

Just when I was feeling very uncertain about my physical condition, here was a friend thinking about me and making plans for the future. I could almost feel the exhilaration of skiing down a mountainside with the snow blowing in my face.

And a golfing friend wrote in jest, "I want you to play in a foursome. After you start to walk again, you'll probably have to take lessons to learn how to play again. Good thing. Maybe they'll correct that miserable swing of yours. Anyway, wanted you to know I was thinking about you."

Countless others expressed more serious thoughts, telling me about their prayers for my healing and a bright future.

Most of All, the Lord ⚓

But most of all, it was liberating to know that the Lord was thinking about me. Many times during those days and repeatedly in some sleepless nights of pain, I claimed that Jeremiah 29:11 promise, "For I know the thoughts that I think toward you." The Hebrew word for "thoughts" can also be translated as "plans." The Lord was thinking about me and had plans for the future.

Especially important during those days, He gave me the gift of hope to claim His promise in the midst of two problems I faced in getting well. One was the nagging pain and the other was an inner ache of depression caused at times by the frustration of being incapacitated. I had known little of either pain or depression before this experience. Now I needed the physical and emotional healing I'd preached about and prayed for in the lives of others for so long.

Hope in Pain

Instead of a quick, easy alleviation of pain, I discovered how to experience the Lord's love in the midst of pain. At first, I prayed that the Lord would simply take the pain away. I'd prayed that for others, and sometimes the Lord had answered by giving them freedom from pain. Apparently, this was not the plan for me in this instance. I had to find Him in the pain.

Really, He found me. He drew me into a more intimate relationship with Himself than I'd ever known before. My hope was in Him and not just in getting rid of the pain. The times of intense pain became redemptive. And then, as the Lord's healing power continued to restore my leg and my whole body, the pain lessened, but not before I'd discovered this deeper experience of His grace. Proverbs 15:30 says, "Good news gives health to the bones." And what is that good news? The Lord will never leave or forsake us and that He is the healer.

Moments of Depression

The discovery I'd made about pain now had to be applied to times when I had an inner aching feeling. This inner ache was caused by my inability to *do* many things I was normally able to handle. At such times my family and friends would say, "Don't worry about that. . . . You've been through a lot and it's just taking time to get well."

You bet it was taking time, time from my primary source of security—performance in my work. I could not preach, be a pastor to my congregation, or produce radio and television programs. All I could do was read my Bible, pray, rest, and just enjoy being alive.

Aha, you've guessed what I'm going to write next. That's exactly what the Lord wanted me to do so I could hear what He'd been trying to tell me for years. I could almost hear Him say, "Lloyd, I love you not for what you *do* but for what you are—My person."

One of the most hopeful things I read while confined to bed was a talk Henri Nouwen gave at Harvard. It was entitled "The Peace That Is Not of This World," and in it he described his experience of moving from being a professor at Harvard teaching the "best and the brightest," to use his words, to a community for handicapped people called Daybreak, near Toronto.

At Daybreak he's called "an assistant." His only assignment, like that of the three others, is to care for six handicapped people in his "family" unit. An epileptic young man named Adam is his special assignment. Nouwen bathes, shaves, dresses, and cares for Adam's needs. After a seizure, Nouwen must bathe and soothe Adam until the trauma is past. And in Adam, he has seen God's unqualified love for a person who can neither produce nor perform.

The reason Dr. Nouwen's experience meant so much to me was because it reminded me that my value to the Lord is not dependent on how much work I do or how many people I reach. Knowing that we are loved just as we are is the assurance in which hope can be experienced. We can't produce hope. It's not our quivering reach to grasp some possibility; it's His mighty grasp on us.

During the months of getting back on my feet, the Lord repeatedly healed the inner ache of frustration by loving me profoundly. With that love, I could accept His promises for the strength and courage I needed.

If It Breaks, I'll Fix It!

When it was time to put weight on my leg and learn to walk again, the surgeon, looking at the x-rays, said, "Put your weight on that leg. It's ready. And if it breaks, I'll fix it."

And, in many ways, that's what the Lord says to us. "I've healed you, now move into the future unafraid. And if anything breaks, I'll fix it."

Several months after surgery, I was back at work— hobbling on a cane and on a limited schedule, to be sure, but way ahead of schedule. Each day there was a little less pain and a little more strength. Among my special memories were the day I walked to the end of our street, the day I went up a flight of stairs, or threw away my cane, or swung a golf club again.

Now, though, a year later, back at full schedule, the unforgettable memory of those days is what I discovered about authentic hope. I wouldn't trade anything for that. The Lord spared my life, healed me, and gave me a new beginning. He gave me Himself.

And that's hope!

Chapter Two

ALWAYS, THERE IS HOPE

Chiseled on the doorway to the parish church of Staunton Harold in Leicestershire, England, are these remarkable words:

In the yeare: 1653
When all things sacred were throughout the Nation
either demolisht or profaned,
Sir Robert Shirley Barronet
founded this church;
Whose singular praise it is
to have done the best things in the worst times
and
to have hoped them in the most calamitous.

To hope "in the most calamitous"—that's the challenging calling of a Christian. It's the motivation for attempting the best of things in what many call the worst of times. Perhaps people in every period of

41

history have had ample reason to think of their years as the worst of times. Ours is certainly no exception.

⚓ A Pall of Hopelessness

A pall of grim hopelessness hangs over us as we move through the closing years of the twentieth century. False hopes have been exposed as unreliable and inadequate. We are not at war, but we all live with the anxiety over the danger of a nuclear war that no one will win. There is angry hatred in Northern Ireland as brother fights brother. The bloody feuding of Arabs and Jews in the Middle East stains the headlines of our daily papers. And the struggle for power in the Third World spreads crippling terror among people who are already suffering from hunger and totalitarian slavery.

At the same time, our confidence in leaders has been smashed. Political and spiritual leaders have been exposed for lack of moral integrity and financial accountability. Social and economic movements once thought to be society's saviors have failed.

"Whom can we trust?" we ask. Political parties flounder for lack of leadership. The economy teeters in the dark shadows of "Black Monday." The church appears more divided than ever and seems devoid of either evangelical zeal or social responsibility.

Meanwhile, many Christians have gone into the closet, not to pray, but to hide. All the negative publicity about some leaders and expressions of Christianity in America has made many people both embarrassed and cautious. Some have become so preoccupied with not being identified with eccentric brands of self-serving Christianity, that there has been little time or energy left to share their own faith with others. At the same time, many Christians hesitate to take a stand and get involved in gigantic social needs in our cities that are still a priority on the Lord's unfinished agenda.

A Pitiful Picture of Hope

The artist G. F. Watts painted a picture of a blindfolded woman with head bowed and holding a lyre, sitting on a sphere we suppose is the world. Only one string of the instrument remains unbroken; only one star shines in the dark sky.

In an effort to interpret his painting for those who might not catch its symbolic meaning, the artist had a one-word sign placed beneath the painting when it was hung in a British art gallery. The word was "hope."

One evening two Cockney cleaning women stood looking at the painting. One, somewhat mystified, wondered, "Hope? Now why would *that* be called hope?"

"Well," the other cleaning woman replied, "I s'pose she's hopin' she ain't gonna fall off!"

Many people today would share that feeling. The one string we have left that we think is hope is frayed and about to break, and we're afraid the world we are sitting on so insecurely has run wild and is out of orbit. We've come to the shocking conclusion that hope based on an innate goodness of people or their ability to solve their own problems is ill-founded—it just doesn't seem to be working.

Our Personal Need for Hope

At the same time, we're all weighed down with staggering personal problems that cause us to feel hopeless.

43

We have more than our share of worry over making ends meet, anxiety about loved ones, and grief over broken or strained relationships. We feel overloaded by stress-pressures and the tension of the never-ending succession of challenges that stretch us beyond our strength and ability to cope.

Added to the daily demands of life are the unanticipated crises that catch us off guard and make us wonder if there's any hope.

A friend of mine confided, "On 1987's Black Monday, in three hours, I lost half of my worth." Another couple who had planned their whole lives around being able to retire comfortably because of carefully arranged investments lost almost everything. "What's there to hope for now?" they asked with discouragement.

During the same week that question was put to me by several different people facing other causes of hopelessness. First it was asked by a man whose wife had just asked for a divorce. Then it came from a woman who had just been told she had cancer. Next it was asked by a young teen-age girl facing an unwanted pregnancy and by a woman nursing her husband through the last stages of Alzheimer's Disease. A pastor who lost his church because of false accusations by a woman who claimed he had made sexual advances felt hopeless in trying to regain his reputation and ministry. Finally, there was a desperate couple whose son had just been diagnosed as having AIDS.

You may be thinking that was an unusual week: six encounters with people suddenly rendered hopeless by the unexpected blows of crises. Not so. In fact, hardly a day of my life goes by without talking to someone whose previously happy life has been invaded by some difficulty or tragedy. Added to these are all the people who are hopelessly resigned to bracing themselves, waiting for the other shoe of some new disappointment to drop.

We become like Snoopy of the Peanuts comic strip. In one of the strips, he is shown in the first frame typing a novel. He starts his story with the words, "It was a dark and stormy night." That's the way Snoopy always begins his stories.

In the next frame, Lucy comes along and berates Snoopy for being dumb and stupid. In no uncertain terms she tells him that any good story opens with "Once upon a time . . ." After giving him a few more put-downs, she walks off.

The final frame shows Snoopy beginning his story again. This time, he types, "Once upon a time, it was a dark and stormy night."

It's easy to get down on ourselves in our dark and stormy times. However we start our stories, we sound the same gloomy note. Most serious of all, however, is the uncertainty of some Christians about exactly how God helps us in our times of need. "Just what can we expect?" we ask.

Is There Always Hope? ⚓

My friend Dave has a flip retort he thoughtlessly uses as a last resort at the end of a discussion of unresolved problems. He gathers up his papers, stands up and says, "Well, there's always hope!"

Is that true? Is there always hope? Well, yes and no. No, hope is not something we have naturally. It can't be humanly induced on demand, even in our most soul-stretching situations.

And yet, there *is* always hope. But true hope is so much more than the facsimile we try to conjure up in times of need. So we are forced to ask, "What is authentic hope?" Before we answer that, though, I want us to consider realistically what hope is not.

⚓ What Hope Is Not

First, *hope is not wishful thinking.* Naturally, we all have wishes for ourselves, for other people, and for the future. These wishes are the product of our human desires, and reflections—our perception of what we think would be best or satisfying· for us. Sometimes our wishful thinking takes the form of fantasies in which we live out on the picture screen of our imaginations the drama of our dreams. All too often, we try to wish some things into existence, and wish some other things away.

When we give people a birthday party we often present them with a birthday cake with lighted candles on top. "Make a wish!" we say. "If you blow out all the candles, your wish will come true."

But as the years go by and there are more candles on the cake, we find it harder to blow out all of them in one try. The same thing happens to our wishing. The years teach us that wishing doesn't necessarily make it so. Life seldom marches to the drumbeat of wishes.

When I was a boy, my family called the Sears Roebuck catalogue "the Wish Book." In my case, the wishes always exceeded what my parents could afford and what would have been good for me. And, of course, when I focused on my wishes, I wasn't hoping. Hope is so much more than a self-induced wishing.

Second, *hope is not yearning.* We often incorrectly use the word "hope" to express our yearning. "Oh, I hope so!" we say, expressing a longing for something to be true or to happen. "Here's hoping," we say in response to a possibility.

Yearning is simply a more intense form of wishing. It's all guts and gusto. It also sets us up for some big disappointments. We waste a lot of energy trying to yearn things into existence. Sometimes yearning even becomes a substitute for prayer.

True hope is so much more than a subjective response to something we want, coupled with the idea that the more we yearn for it the better are our chances of getting it. But constant disappointment with that facsimile of hope gets us down on what we think is hope. Things, people, plans, and ideas of what we think might be best for us can be very unreliable grounds for hope.

Unfortunately, our yearning is too seldom refined by deep conversations with God. We want what we want, and long for it. When something we longed for happens, we take the credit. When it doesn't, we assume the blame by saying that we simply didn't want it badly enough.

G. K. Chesterton once said, "There are no rules of architecture for castles in the clouds." Indeed not. They are drafted to the specifications of our limited ideas of what we think would be best for us.

That's just the problem. Our castles of yearning are built without the solid foundation of guidance from the Lord. And only He can be the reliable architect for the future of our lives.

Henry David Thoreau wisely wrote:

If you build castles in the air
Your work need not be lost.
That's where they should be.
Now put foundations under them.

Third, *hope is not simply cheery optimism.* Hope certainly can produce an optimistic attitude, but an optimistic attitude is no substitute for true hope.

Richard Rodgers wrote a song especially for Mary Martin to sing in *South Pacific.* We all know the lyrics that begin, "I'm only a cockeyed optimist." What some may not know is that Mary doesn't just sing about the hope she "can't get out of her head"; she really has hope that enables her optimism. It's not just optimism that has gotten her through difficult times.

Optimism and hope are often confused. But optimism which is not based on God's promises, power, and faithfulness fades under the pressure of disappointments.

Some people have sunny dispositions because of positive conditioning. Often that's paraded as hope. But a flip repeating of the words "things work out for the best" is a far cry from authentic hope.

Sir Thomas Lipton expressed neither praise to God nor modesty about himself when he said, "I'm the world's greatest optimist. I'm proud of the distinction. There is something buoyant and healthy about being an optimist. It is because of optimism that I have gone through life smiling. I am always in good humor and good fettle. Dr. Optimist is the finest chap in any city in our country. Just try a course of his treatment. It works wonders, and this doctor charges no fees."

The strength of optimism, however, like the tea bags named in Sir Lipton's honor, is not tested until it gets into hot water. To extend the metaphor—optimism alone produces a weak, unstimulating brew! It takes more than optimism that "things are getting better and better every day in every way" to be a survivor in life as you and I know it. We need virile, lasting hope for that. "So don't just tell me what hope is not," you say. "If it isn't frail wish-dreaming, or unproductive yearning, or unfounded optimism, what is it?"

What Hope Is

In the Old Testament, mainly two Hebrew words are used for hope. One simply means waiting for what is ahead. The other, from the root meaning "cord" or "rope," denotes more of a tense or eager expectation.

The hope of the faithful in the Old Testament is closely connected to the idea of trust. And God—Yahweh—is the object, focus and guarantor of this hope. It is rooted and grounded in His truth, righteousness and mercy and in expectation of His intervention. Hope in the Old Testament is an attitude of submission to God based on an assurance that He would keep His promises to His people. This is refined into a specific anticipation of the coming of the Messiah, the new covenant and His reign in glory.

In the New Testament, the basis of hope is that the Messiah has come in the person of Jesus of Nazareth. In Him the kingdom of God, His reign and rule, has been established. Christ's life, message, atonement for the sins of the world, and resurrection are now the basis of hope.

The living Christ not only is the object of hope, but the One who engenders it. Lasting hope is created and sustained by the indwelling Christ in believers and by His presence in the church. Those who have authentic hope for this life and eternity are those who have received the gift of faith to trust Christ as Savior and Lord, have experienced a rebirth to new life and have received the infilling of His Spirit.

⚓ Hope Is a Gift

Here, then, is a definition of authentic hope. Hope is a gift of God through Christ that produces a confident, unshakable trust in His faithfulness, and a vibrant expectation of His timely interventions in keeping with His gracious promises to us. Authentic hope is always a by-product of a personal relationship with God. It comes from knowing God.

There's nothing more important than knowing God. To know Him and to have a heart for Him is our greatest privilege and our most urgent need. Intimate personal knowledge of God is also to be our primary desire and our burning passion. "Thus says the Lord: Let not the wise man glory in his wisdom, let not the mighty man glory in his might, let not the rich man glory in his riches; but let him who glories glory in this, that he understands and knows Me, that I am the Lord, exercising loving-kindness, judgment and righteousness in the earth. For in these I delight, says the Lord" (Jer. 9:23–24).

⚓ Awesome!

That's awesome! God, who knows all about us, wants us to know Him. He is the God of all hope. With hope He created us to know and love Him, and Christ came to provide a lasting basis for our hope. As the divine Son of God in human flesh, Jesus exposed in His own life the essence of hope rooted in the love and faithfulness of God the Father. With complete trust that God would intervene with the resurrection, Christ our Savior went to the cross to suffer for our sins. Then, in the ultimate miracle of all time, God raised Him from the dead. Now Christ is our risen, reigning Lord. Emmanuel, God with us, forever.

Through His Spirit God convinces us that we are loved unreservedly, that we are forgiven through the cross of Christ, and that He will never leave or forsake us. He gives us the gift of faith to accept His atoning death for us and the willingness to be filled with His Spirit. Then He gives us the desire to seek and follow His guidance. We feel confident expectation of His enabling power for our daily problems and challenges. It is then that hope begins to grow in us.

A Living Hope

Near the end of his life, Peter referred to this kind of hope as a *living* hope. But the apostle's experience of this quality of hope had not come easily. That's why his witness is so invaluable to us.

Peter had been with Christ all through His hope-inspiring ministry. He felt intensely the impact of the Master's confidence in him and what he could become. Life with Jesus had been thrilling and exhilarating. Peter could remember the awesome moment when he was sure that Jesus was the Messiah, the Son of the Living God. "You shall be called Peter," Jesus had said, "and on this rock I will build My church" (Matt. 16:18). Peter's human expectation had been filled with a strange new hope. But it didn't last. During Jesus' trial, Peter's hope wavered, and he denied his Lord. And then when He was crucified, all of Peter's new-found hope died with the Master he had loved and followed.

An excruciating hopelessness gripped Peter and the other disciples as they sat in shocked silence in the Upper Room following the crucifixion. The faint stirrings of hope they had experienced were gone now, and in their place came the same old fears and anxieties they had known before He had called them. We can empathize with their despair.

> We did not dare to breathe a prayer
> Or give our anguish scope.
> Something was dead in all of us
> And what was dead was hope.[1]

But now capture the awesome wonder Peter felt when Mary burst into the Upper Room with the astounding news that Jesus had risen from the dead and she had talked with Him. Peter's feet couldn't carry him fast enough as he raced to the tomb to see for himself. It was true!

Then later in the day the risen Christ appeared to the disciples in the Upper Room. God had intervened and raised Jesus from the dead. In the presence of the risen Lord, the same hope Peter had felt before began to stir again.

Repeated appearances by the living Christ in the days following His resurrection instigated a momentary experience of hope in Peter and the disciples. Only in the presence of the Lord did they sense it. But then the Lord told them that He was going away.

On hearing that Peter's heart sank again. "No Lord, no hope," he thought. But Jesus promised to return. And when He did, the disciples would receive power— a promise worth waiting for.

It happened on the day of Pentecost. Peter and the disciples were infilled with Christ's Spirit. Now with the gift of His indwelling Spirit, all that He had said earlier made sense. Peter looked back at the cross, and he understood the cosmic atonement for his sins and the sins of the whole world that had taken place there. God has been faithful to His promise in raising Jesus from the dead. The assurance of that ultimate miracle of intervention made Peter sure that God was more than adequate to invade his times of deepest need through the presence and power of the reigning Christ.

Furthermore, most amazing of all, Peter understood that the resurrection had happened to him. He had been raised up out of the grave of his old vacillating, inadequate, and anxious self to a new life of boldness, courage, and vision. Peter was the new man Christ had promised he would become. And with His Spirit living in him, he had an indefatigable hope no one could dissuade and no adversity could destroy.

After years of having that hope tested and refined by persecution, imprisonment and suffering, Peter wrote these encouraging words to his fellow Christians: "Blessed be the God and Father of our Lord Jesus Christ, *who according to His abundant mercy has begotten us again to a living hope* through the resurrection of Jesus Christ from the dead, to an inheritance incorruptible and undefiled that does not fade away, reserved in heaven for you" (1 Pet. 1:3-4, italics added). In this stirring confession, Peter reminds us of the source of the distinctive quality of our hope and gives us the secret of how to experience hope while at the same time assuring us of the security of true hope's lasting power.

⚓ A Distinctive Quality

Yes, our hope is a living hope. It has unquenchable zest and vitality. It is not dependent on conditions or circumstance. And it's not just an idea or just a feeling.

The source of our hope is the mercy of God. "According to His abundant mercy . . ." Grace, unqualified love, is God's nature. His mercy is His grace reaching out to us in our alienation from Him. Mercifully, God came in His Son to reconcile us to Himself. With sublime mercy, He raised Christ from the dead, and through the Holy Spirit He is with us forever. The mercy of God in Christ has defeated everything that previously had diminished the capacity to hope—sin, despair, discouragement, helplessness, and the tyranny of fear and death.

Amy Carmichael said, "We cannot fill ourselves with hope; we have no wells of hope within us. But God has; just as He is the God of love, so that we can pray, 'Love through me, Love of God,' so He is the God of Hope, and we can pray, 'Hope through me, Hope of God.'" And He does that through His Son, whose Spirit He sends into our hearts.

At this point you may be wondering, "Many people could agree with all you've said about the mercy of God in Christ and still find it difficult to hope. Why is this?"

54

The Secret ⚓

The secret of experiencing living hope is in what Peter describes as being "begotten again." The Greek word literally means "born again, experiencing a rebirth." Real hope is the precious possession of the twice born.

Our first physical birth took place as a result of our conception in our mother's womb. Spiritual birth happens in a similar way. We are mercifully given the gift of faith to believe in Christ and commit our lives to Him. He begins to grow within us. Christ's death and resurrection are actually repeated in us. As we surrender our lives to Him, we die to ourselves—our pride, self-centeredness, plans and purposes. Then the miracle of the resurrection takes place in us. We are raised up to a whole new dimension of living filled with Christ—His mind, His character, His power.

Peter goes on later in the first chapter of his first epistle to tell us about the assurance of our status and security. "Having been born again, not of corruptible seed but incorruptible, through the word of God which lives and abides forever . . ." (1 Pet. 1:23). The implanted word is Christ Himself. When we receive Him, we grow into His likeness, develop Christ-centered personalities, experience His patience, see things from His point of view and are able to face the uncertainties of life with His hope surging within us.

When this happens, the fear of death no longer has power over us. We are alive forever. Our physical death will be a further experience of resurrection. The inheritance of being made like Christ will be even more fully consummated in heaven.

Now we can see why being born again is so essential to experiencing living hope. Hope Himself takes up residence in our hearts. Our hope has life to it because our living Lord creates it.

⚓ A Constantly Renewed Experience

Being born again to a living hope, though, is not a once-done event, but a constantly renewed experience. Recently, at a conference, a man tried to take my spiritual pulse. "Dr. Ogilvie, when were you born again?" he demanded. My reply startled him, "Well," I said, "about thirty-seven years ago, many times through the years and, as a matter of fact, just this morning!"

"No, you don't understand," he persisted. "When were you filled with Jesus?" Again my answer was not what he expected to hear. "My friend, I was filled with Christ's indwelling Spirit when I first committed my life to Him. But every day, every hour, I find that life's challenges force me to confess my inadequacy and the need to open myself to a fresh filling of the Lord's power."

Many committed Christians who would claim a rebirth experience find that crises expose their need for hope. All too often we depend on our previous experiences of Christ rather than our present experience of His hope-inspiring Spirit. It's then that we learn hope is not something we produce but something He provides.

That's what happened to me after my fall in Scotland while I was trying to drag myself to safety. I couldn't muster up the hope I needed. But a surrender of the impossibilities opened me to trust the Lord more than ever. In a sense I was reborn once again to living, lively hope. My urgent need drove me to draw on my spiritual inheritance. Fortunately, the resources of that inheritance of hope are limitless. They can never be depleted.

Where There's Hope, There's Life

So often we hear the trite phrase, "Where there's life, there's hope." It's used to suggest that as long as our pulse is beating, our lungs have breath in them and there's still life in our brains, there's hope.

I was happy recently to find the source of that shallow shibboleth. John Gay, 1685–1732, first wrote it in a grim poem called "The Sick Man and the Angel."

> Where there's life, there's hope, he cried.
> Then why such haste? So groaned and died.

Actually, the truth is: where there's hope, there's life. The gift of hope enables us to live expectantly, knowing that Christ is in charge. Nothing can happen that He won't use to deepen His relationship with us. And in addition, He will give us supernatural strength and courage, in ways we could not imagine or program. He will provide the three things we need most in crises: trust, guidance and inspiration.

Trust

The other day I reread the ninth chapter of Isaiah. The words of the prophet leaped off the page, "The government will be upon His shoulder . . . and of the increase of His government and peace there will be no end . . ." (Isa. 9:6–7).

I wondered, is the government of my life upon the shoulders of the reigning Christ? Have I intentionally placed the concerns, challenges, people and the projects of my life on Him for His management? Do I want Him to take charge?

Having asked those questions, I sat back in my chair and laughed out loud. How stupid to live with a mess of stress when the Savior of the world has offered to run my life. He has limitless resources: all power in heaven and earth, authority to arrange circumstances, people to deploy to help, and knowledge of the future. Best of all, He gives us Himself—unfailing Friend, gracious Comforter, and forgiving Savior. The assurance of Christ's intervention gives us hope.

Guidance

Christ is also our guide. Sometimes things in life just don't make sense. We thrash about with questions of why and when and how. And yet Christ has promised to give us all the guidance we need to know and do His will. As we reflect on the past, we realize He's given us whatever wisdom we've required for each day. That gives us living hope for our tomorrows.

John Oxenham's words express this confidence in the interpretive ministry of Christ, our hope:

> Not for one single day
> Can I discern the way,
> But this I surely know:
> Who gives the day

Will show the way,
So I securely go.[2]

Inspiration ⚓

Confidence in Jesus Christ is directly dependent on receiving His inspiration. But He never does that from a lofty distance. Inspiration means being "inspirited," being given a spirit. For a Christian, that means Christ's invasion into our minds, emotions and wills. In attentive prayer He gives us wisdom and insight. He guides us to just the right passages of Scripture. And He uses trusted friends to share the truth we need at a particular time.

Christ also inspires us emotionally. He helps us retrace our down moods to the root in either self-incrimination or blame of others. Once the root is exposed, He offers us forgiveness for what we've done and the freedom to forgive what's been done to us.

Our hope in Christ's inspiration also includes our wills. Think of the times we needed the willingness to do what we knew He had guided and mysteriously we began to want what He wanted with compelling desire. Or remember those times when you needed to say "no" or faced a beguiling temptation and He gave the courage to resist. At the same time, all of us are facing the tasks and challenges of life. Will Christ give us the enthusiasm and will to tackle them? Yes! He has promised and we can trust Him.

Hope makes us bold and daring. It broadens our horizons to include challenges we'd never attempt on our own. We no longer plan according to what we can do but what Christ has shown us He is ready and able to do through us.

⚓ He Gives What He Asks

But the great good news of the gospel is that the Lord asks from us only what He offers to give to us. Hope is no exception. He knows how desperately we need hope to live confidently and courageously in a time like ours.

This is not a time to say to one another, "You gotta have hope!" Or to ourselves, "You need to try to be more hopeful." But it is time to recognize that it's humanly impossible to have hope except as a gift from the One who is hope.

Paul put it succinctly when he wrote to his young friend Timothy, "The Lord Jesus Christ, our hope . . ." (1 Tim. 1:1). Not just the object of hope but the Spirit of Hope within us.

The basis of hope is both what Christ has done for us in the cross and resurrection and in His presence and power with us in our problems and needs. The sure evidence of hope is Christ in our hearts.

NOTES

1. Oscar Wilde, *The Ballad of Reading Gaol* (1898), III. 31.
2. John Oxenham (1852–1941), *Bees and Amber*. Used by permission of Desmond Dunkerley.

Chapter Three

MIND
YOUR HEAD
AND
SERVE THE KING!

Andrew and Fiona, a sprightly old Scots couple, are the proud caretakers of their clan's castle in the Highlands of Scotland.

When I visited them prior to my accident, my host was most eager to show me his display of antique pieces of armor he had collected through the years. I was particularly impressed with the array of helmets representing various periods of ancient Scottish history.

As I examined the carefully hammered metal of one of these helmets, Andrew explained, "The helmet was one of the most important parts of a suit of armor. It protected the warrior's head and his brain. A wound or blow to the head would take him out of battle. He had to think clearly to serve his king. Under surprise attack, it was important to get the helmet on, or you might not get the rest on."

Over the shelf on which Andrew had arranged the   63

helmets in historical order, he had placed a placard with the words of a centuries-old motto. It read, "Mine Yer Heid an' Serv' tha King!"

That would be a good motto for us as we press on to claim the promise of a future and a hope. Once we have discovered that Christ Himself is hope, the next step is to allow Him to control and guide our thinking.

⚓ A Motto for Hopeful Thinkers

We are called to be hopeful thinkers. To live out that calling our motto needs to be, "Mind your thinking and serve Christ your King!"

What we think about controls our outlook on life— our attitudes, how we look at the problems and potentials of life, our relationships, and what we dare to expect that the Lord can do to help us. In between the impact of what's happening to and around us there is a split-second mental response that triggers how we perceive things, how we feel, and how we react.

Our thinking determines how well we will survive in a battle we must fight all of our lives. There can never be a truce. This battle is with discouragement, the antagonist of hope. It's one of the most deadly weapons of the force of evil.

⚓ Our Battle with Discouragement

We all experience discouragement at times. Some seldom are free of the spiritual malaise. Perhaps you are suffering from discouragement right now. Or maybe this debilitating virus has attacked your thinking in the past and you feel ill prepared for the next encounter with it. And all of us are deeply concerned about loved ones, friends, or people at work who so often are immobilized by discouragement. We long to help them. We wish we could find a sure cure that would work for us so we could share it with them.

The battleground of our warfare with discouragement is in our minds. It's in our thinking that we win or lose the battle. For that battle the Lord has provided a very crucial piece of armor. There's just no way we can survive without it. This strategic piece of battle gear must be reissued every morning by the Lord. We dare not get out of bed, much less live throughout any day, without being refitted with it. It is the hopeful thinker's most invaluable possession. The apostle Paul calls it the helmet of hope.

In this chapter, I want to share how I rediscovered the protective power of this helmet of hope. Then I will show how we can win in the battle with the discouragement caused by negative thinking around us and by the neutralizing efforts of the forces of evil. Then in the next chapter we will consider the hopeful thinkers' prayer. All this is so we can "mind our thinking and serve our King"!

The Helmet of Hope

I rediscovered the helmet of hope during the long months of recovery from my crushed leg. One day, when the pain was particularly acute and the waiting to get back on my feet again seemed endless, I was feeling discouraged. Knowing from experience that feelings and attitudes follow thought, I knew I had to get my thinking straight again. So, toward the end of that "down" day of struggle, I picked up my Bible and looked for a fresh word of encouragement from the Lord. I was not disappointed.

While I was convalescing, I had been reading Paul's first letter to the Thessalonians, written to give the new Christians strength and courage for their spiritual battles. My reading that evening brought me to chapter five. Verse eight leaped off the page and riveted my attention. Though I had read and preached on that verse many times through the years, now it gripped me as if I were reading it for the first time. "Putting on the breastplate of faith and love, and as a helmet the hope of salvation."

In the midst of pain and discouragement I was feeling, I knew I needed both the helmet to protect my thinking and the breastplate to guard my attitudes. While I was reflecting on Paul's words, I remembered my visit to Andrew's weaponry room and his explanation that under surprise attack a soldier needed to get his helmet on first, before putting on the rest of his armor. There was no doubt about it—I was under surprise attack and needed to be equipped for the spiritual battle. I spent a long time thinking about the helmet of hope and how it could work in my time of need.

⚓ Protection of the Mind

What a medieval warrior's helmet of armor did to protect his head, the spiritual helmet of hope does to shield our minds. It guards our thinking against the invasion of thoughts of discouragement.

We become discouraged when we entertain as honored guests in our mind thoughts instigated by the invading, clamoring tribe of disappointment, impatience, and frustration. That whole tribe was working me over at the end of that difficult day. I needed to put on the helmet of hope.

Putting on the Helmet ⚓

To put on this protective helmet, I took a prolonged time of prayer before I went to sleep. I urgently needed a fresh invasion of hope, and I confessed my need to the Lord during my prayer time. But I didn't just ask for hope, for I've discovered that the gift of authentic hope is always a subjective response to the objective power of salvation. That's why Paul didn't challenge the Thessalonians just to put on a helmet of hope, but the helmet of the hope of salvation.

So I focused my mind on the splendor of the cornucopian word that Paul used for salvation. It means deliverance, wholeness, and healing. And I needed a renewed experience of all three. Put simply, salvation is everything Christ has done in the past, is anxious to do for us now, and will do for us in the future.

Paul uses the past, present, and future tenses when he talks about salvation in his letters. In Ephesians he says, "For by grace you have been saved through faith" (2:8). Christ delivered us from our sins on the cross. When we receive the gift of faith and commit our lives to Him as our Lord and Savior, we were forgiven and given hope.

Then in writing to his friends in Corinth, Paul speaks of Christians as those "who are being saved" (1 Cor. 1:18). Day by day we experience the fresh wonder of belonging to Christ, and our hope increases.

But that's not all—we will be saved. We need have no fear of what will happen to us in the future, in our death, or where we will spend eternity. That's the conviction Paul shares with the Roman Christians when he writes, "Much more then, having now been justified by His blood, we shall be saved from wrath through Him" (Rom. 5:9).

⚓ Alive with Hope

During my "down moments" I thought about all that Christ meant to me, and my mind came alive with hope. The helmet of hope of salvation was being repositioned over my thinking, and that enabled me to claim Christ's healing and wholeness for my body. Discouraging thoughts were displaced with thoughts of trust and confidence in Christ's power. In this process He was delivering me from worry over the past, anxiety over my present needs, and fear about the future.

I prayed, "Lord, take possession of my thinking. Refocus my mind on what you have done for me. Inspire my imagination with your vision for me as a healed and whole person. Thank you for making me a hopeful thinker again." He answered my prayer. I went to sleep and slept with profound peace.

You can be sure that the next morning I put on the helmet of hope of salvation the moment I awoke rather than waiting to put it on later in the day, in the midst of the battle. I had relearned a difficult lesson. I can't make it through any day without the protection of the helmet of hope.

No one can. We are not naturally hopeful thinkers. We must live each day with our minds connected to the

68

flow of the current of Christ's mind rather than the rundown batteries of our previous experiences of His hope. We need His perspective and vision for every challenge and opportunity all through the day. And He is ready to show us His plan for us in our relationships and in our problems. That, along with His promise to continue to abide in our minds, gives us hope. We do not hope that His promise might be fulfilled; we hope because it is *being fulfilled* moment by moment.

The Litmus Test

Do you think of yourself as a hopeful thinker? Or for a more accurate test—would the people in your family, your friends at church or where you work call you a hopeful thinker? And to be even more specific, do you focus your mind each day on the challenges and opportunities that are yours? Is your thinking filled with confident hope in what the Lord is able to do?

When I honestly answer these questions myself, I realize how much I need the helmet of hope every day to serve Christ the King.

Not Easy

It's not easy being a hopeful thinker in a world that is doing all it can, night and day, to infect our minds with discouragement. There are negative, hopeless thinkers all around us—people who look at life with a limited perspective. Over the years, they have become disappointed with themselves and others. Life hasn't turned out the way they had planned. Unfortunately, their grim view of the future is contagious.

But there's another reason we need to put on the helmet of hope. There's a pervasive force of evil in the world. Call it what you will—the force of evil, the evil one, Satan—we have a formidable enemy who seeks to invade our thinking with discouragement.

⚓ The Neutralizer

Satan is the neutralizer. You may think that's too benign a title. Look again at the definition of neutralize. It means to counteract or destroy by an opposing force or influence; to nullify or counterbalance; to render powerless. In military terms, neutralize means to make an enemy base, outpost, or city incapable of effective action.

Now perhaps you can understand why "the neutralizer" is an appropriate title for Satan. He seeks to counteract Christ's positive conditioning of our thinking. His goal is to get us out of the spiritual battle. He is too clever to launch a frontal attack. Instead he sneaks behind the lines of our defenses, tries to minimize our vision, and causes us to be satisfied with the mediocre —and even base—things in life. His strategy is to get us to settle for less than the best the Lord wants us to have, to distract us from our King's optimal plan for us, the people around us, the church, our communities, and our nation.

⚓ Time for Reflection

Let's reflect on that for a moment.

Can you remember a time when you wanted to accomplish something really important, but before you'd barely got started, you were engulfed with thoughts of failure, feelings that you probably wouldn't succeed?

Or, have you ever felt motivated to say or do something to express your love and caring for someone but then didn't carry out your intentions because you let yourself be discouraged by the thought that your gesture probably wouldn't be appreciated or accepted?

Have you ever tried to break a bad habit, but your first attempts were invaded by the thought that you'd not be able to keep your resolve?

And in living out your faith, do you find that you make yourself grand promises only to find yourself procrastinating with excuses like "Well, nobody's perfect," or "Everyone else is compromising; why be so hard on myself?" Even further, have you ever consciously done something you know is wrong and then passed it off with the excuse "Oh well, it won't really make a difference!"

If you're married, have you ever thought your marriage had stalled on a plateau and might never improve? Have you ever said to yourself, "Well, that's just the way he is, and I'll have to bear it"? Or, "She's never going to change. But why bother? Most people don't have a really happy marriage"?

As parents, our thinking about our children also can be invaded by disappointment and discouragement. At times our thoughts are flooded with worry and anxiety about their future or whether they'll make it through the painful periods of growing up. Sometimes our thinking can be muddled by thoughts of our own failure as parents.

Feelings of discouragement and failure can cloud our relationships with friends or people at work. We find it easy to be critical, jealous, or suspicious of them, even to the extent of minimizing their abilities or potential. We may even have let our negative thoughts about them cause us to gossip or promote dissension among them.

And now think about the church. What do you expect? Is your vision for what it can become limited in any way? If all the members of your church had your level of commitment, involvement, and stewardship, what kind of church would it be?

With regard to involvement in community needs, do you have depreciating thoughts like, "What can I do? My efforts would be like irrigating the desert with a tea cup."

All such thoughts may be the neutralizer's minimizing influence. And even if we've thought them up ourselves, we're playing right into his hands. Satan is the debilitator, the reductionist, and original put-down artist.

Now, I want to make it very clear that I don't believe that Satan can possess the life of a Christian. But I am convinced that it is possible for us to be vulnerable to his neutralizing influence in our thinking.

⚓ Simon Peter, For Example

That happened to Simon Peter. After Jesus told the disciples about His coming death on the cross, Peter took the Master aside and actually rebuked Him. "Far be it from You, Lord," Peter said sharply; "this shall not happen to You!" (Matt. 16:22).

Jesus' response is startling. "Get behind Me, Satan! You are an offense to Me, for you are not mindful of the things of God, but the things of men" (Matt. 16:23).

The word "mindful" leaps out of Jesus' incisive response. Peter's thinking was being distorted. His
thoughts had been influenced by the neutralizer who
wanted to dissuade Jesus from the cross at all cost.

Satan had used Peter's confused mixture of affection
for Jesus and fear for his own safety to motivate the
imperious thought that he could control the Master's
destiny. But Jesus recognized the source. He had confronted the neutralizer in the wilderness temptation
prior to beginning His ministry.

You will recall how Satan had tried to neutralize
Jesus' calling to be the Bread of Life by telling Him to
turn stones into bread to meet the *immediate* physical
hungers of people. Next Satan tried to tempt Jesus with
the *expedient* by casting himself down from the pinna-
cle of the temple and being miraculously saved from
death. Finally, Satan tempted Jesus with *temporary* rec-
ognition and adulation of the kingdoms of the world
and their glory. All Jesus had to do was to fall down
and worship Satan.

To all of this Jesus simply said, "Away with you, Satan! For it is written, 'You shall worship the Lord your
God, and Him only shall you serve'" (Matt. 4:10). The
Hope of the world had resisted Satan's influence to
accept the immediate, the expedient, and the temporary
instead of the cross. Matthew tells us, "Then the devil
left Him, and behold, angels came and ministered to
Him" (Matt. 4:11).

But the neutralizer did not give up. He persisted
with his effort to influence Jesus' enemies, the vacillating minds of the disciples, and the countless others
who resisted Jesus' call to commitment. The Master
knew what was happening. He warned His disciples

about the neutralizer and prayed for them—especially for Simon Peter. "Simon, Simon! Indeed, Satan has asked for you, that he may sift you like wheat. But I have prayed for you, that your faith should not fail; and when you have returned to me, strengthen your brethren" (Luke 22:31–32). Jesus understood the battle going on in Peter's mind.

The night before Jesus was crucified, He prayed for His disciples and followers in all generations—for you and me. "I do not pray that You should take them out of the world," Jesus prayed to the Father, "but that You should keep them from the evil one. They are not of the world, just as I am not of the world. Sanctify them by Your truth. Your word is truth. As You sent Me into the world, I also have sent them into the world. And for their sakes, I sanctify Myself that they also may be sanctified by the truth" (John 17:15–19).

Then Jesus went to the cross as the Father's answer to this prayer. The word "sanctify" means to consecrate, to set apart for God's purpose. Jesus consecrated Himself to confront Satan on Calvary and wrench humankind from his grip. As our Savior, Christ suffered not only to accomplish ultimate atonement for our sins, but also to strip Satan of his power.

I can remember vividly how James Stewart, beloved professor in my graduate student days and friend through the years, claimed this victory. "If evil at its overwhelming worst has already been met and mastered, as in Jesus Christ it has; if God has got His hands on this baffling mystery of suffering in its direct, most defiant form, and turned its most awful triumph into uttermost, irrevocable defeat—if that in fact has happened, and on that scale, are you to say it cannot happen on the infinitely lesser scale of your own life by union with Christ through faith? In heartbreaking things which happen to us, those physical pains, those mental agonies, those spiritual midnights of the soul, we are 'more than conquerors,' not through our own valor or stoic resolution, not through a creed or code or philosophy, but 'through Him who loved us'— through the thrust and pressure of the invading grace of Christ."

Hope for Discouragement

As we attempt to battle our way through the daily routines, we make a great effort to try to get life together so that we'll have a trouble-free existence. We long for a time when we will have solved all our problems and will be free of concerns. It never happens quite that way, though, and we become discouraged. The neutralizer tempts us with self-condemnation because we haven't done it better. That makes us vulnerable to the deeper temptation to think that no matter what we do, it won't make any difference.

But Christ leads us out of that self-defeating kind of thinking. He focuses our minds on what He wants us to do and gives us the assurance that He will provide the strength we need to accomplish it to His glory. He is the eternal maximizer who helps us confront the minimizing efforts of the neutralizer.

John Henry Jowett expressed it this way: "Hope is a splendid helmet, firmly covering the head and defending all thoughts and purposes and visions from the subtle assaults of the evil one. The helmet of hope is one of the best protections against 'losing one's head'; it is

75

the best security against all attacks made on the mind by small but deadly fears; it is the only effective safeguard against petty but deadly compromise. Far away the best defense against all sorts of mental vagrancy and distraction is to have the executive chambers of the life encircled and possessed by strong and brilliant hope."

That's why Satan cowers at the name of Jesus and slinks away when we claim the cross as our assurance of salvation. The neutralizer cannot penetrate the insulating strength of our protective helmet of the hope of salvation.

So mind your head and serve the King!

Chapter Four

THE HOPEFUL THINKERS' PRAYER

Recently I attended a banquet of British veterans of a World War II commando unit. It was held in honor of their chaplain whom they fondly called "Padre." Before the dinner was served, the master of ceremonies asked the chaplain to pray. In introducing the chaplain, he recalled a request they had made often during the dark days of the invasion of France, "Padre, give us a prayer for the battle." Warmly and with deep affection, the master of ceremonies said to the elderly clergyman, "Come now, Padre, and once again give us a prayer for the battle!"

After receiving thunderous applause, the clergyman wisely reminded the men that living out their faith today is an even greater battle than they had fought together during the war. Then he prayed a magnificent prayer for strength and courage for life's struggles in these closing days of the twentieth century.

⚓ **The Hopeful Thinkers' Prayer**

When Jesus' disciples asked Him to teach them to pray, He gave them a prayer that safeguards the spiritual warrior's mind and really contains the protective layers of the helmet of hope we've been talking about. Traditionally, this prayer has been called The Lord's Prayer (Matt. 6:9–13). It is that, for the Lord Jesus certainly lived every petition of it to the fullest. But this prayer could also be called the Disciples' prayer, for it is only as Christ's disciples that we can pray the bold petitions contained in this awesome prayer.

I'd like to give this prayer a different title, though. It's really "The Hopeful Thinkers' Prayer for Spiritual Warfare." The six petitions need to be prayed intentionally as we put on our helmet of hope. They will revolutionize our thinking and give us hope in discouraging times. And the secret of living these petitions is that the One who taught us to pray them has been delegated by the Father to be with us to answer them. I want to explain each in that illuminating light.

⚓ **The Miracle of the Ordinary**

When we pray "Hallowed be Your name," we are really claiming a miracle in the ordinary. We are asking that all of life be filled with God's name, that is, with His presence and power. The word "hallowed" comes from the root word "holy" and refers to the manifestation or evidence of God's holiness. The petition "hallowed be thy name" uses the passive voice of the verb. We do not do the hallowing; rather the hallowing is something God does to us and around us. We can't make God more holy than He is. What we can do is ask Him to manifest or show His holy presence and power.

As we pray this petition, we mean that we claim every moment, relationship, and situation in life as His gift. They are holy because they belong to Him. That immediately changes our thinking. Instead of living in the past or looking to the future, "now" becomes the most important moment of our lives. We can experience what the eighteenth-century Jesuit Jean-Pierre de Caussarde called "the sacrament of the present moment." The Lord wants to bless every second with His holy presence and guidance in whatever happens to us.

Extraordinary Living

That makes for extraordinary living. My friend Tom, a deeply committed Christian director in television, has discovered that marvelous truth. Quite often when I see him at the end of a busy day, I ask him, "So, how was your day?" And I can always count on this response —"Extraordinary!"

One evening I had to ask. "Tom, you always say that. Is every day really extraordinary?"

His response was a classic. "Lloyd, just to enjoy to the fullest the ordinary is an extraordinary experience! I'm just an ordinary guy, surrounded by ordinary people, doing what becomes ordinary after awhile. I've decided not to miss the joy by constantly searching for some thrill. When I look for what the Lord is doing in the ordinary and commit myself to live in the now, I don't get discouraged. Sorry to preach to a preacher, but you asked. Anyhow, that's why I always say, 'Extraordinary!' when anyone asks me about my day."

⚓ Hallowed Thinking

That's "hallowed thinking." When we pray "Hallowed be Your name," we are asking God to fill us with His holy presence and power. The hallowing of all life as sacred begins in our minds and hearts. God wants to hallow us with the Spirit of Christ. He wants to make us like Christ in our thinking, our character, our personality, and our attitudes. And He has sent Christ to live in us to make that possible.

"Because you are sons," Paul says, "God has sent forth the Spirit of His Son into your hearts, crying out, 'Abba, Father!'" (Gal 4:6). Once that happens, we look at the world around us, at people and at circumstances, through the eyes of Christ. Then we can resign from trying to run our own lives and we can live in the joy of the now. Discouragement over the past or over our plans for the future begins to fade away in the enjoyment of life in the present.

Horatius Bonar has given us a prayer to pray as we claim the hallowing of every moment. I've prayed it often as I begin a new day.

> Fill Thou my life, O Lord my God,
>   In every part with praise,
> That my whole being may proclaim
>   Thy being and Thy ways.
>
> Not for the lip of praise alone,
>   Nor e'en the praising heart
> I ask, but for a life made up
>   Of praise in every part.
>
> So shall each fear, and each fret, each care
>   Be turned into a song;

And every winding of the way
    The echo shall prolong.

No part of day or night
    From sacredness be free:
But all my life, in every step,
    Be fellowship with Thee.[1]

When we begin our day with thoughts like that, everything is transformed. We accept the day as a precious gift from God. As we bathe, we praise the Lord for our bodies. When we eat, we glorify Him for His provision. Each person we meet is honored and affirmed as a special present from our Lord wrapped up in unique wrappings of his or her personality. We think of our work as a privilege rather than a tiresome burden. Old things are done with new enthusiasm, and problems are met with gusto rather than grimness. We know that by facing them with the Lord's help we will discover more of His wisdom and grace.

One morning, as a friend of mine said good-by to his wife before going off to work, she said, "Just give me an ordinary kiss this morning." He replied, "An ordinary kiss?! There is no such thing as an ordinary kiss. Short or long, every kiss from you is extraordinary!" They both laughed, hugged and kissed and went on to the opportunities the day held for each of them.

An extraordinary life is made up of millions of what seem like ordinary moments. Expectation of the manifestation of the Lord's presence and power, the hallowing of all of life, seals us against the invading thoughts of discouragement.

83

⚓ **God's Strategy for Our Lives**

Another layer of our helmet of hope is laminated over our thinking when we pray the next petition of the Hopeful Thinkers' Prayer—"Your Kingdom come, Your will be done on earth as it is in heaven."

This petition opens us to the extraordinary quality of life we just described. God has a strategy for our lives. It is to live every moment in His kingdom here and now with one goal in mind—to know and do His will in every compartment of our lives and in every relationship.

Like the "hallowing" of life, this petition is a gift from God. He is the source of liberating hope. We don't have to create God's kingdom, and most certainly knowledge of the will of God is not meant to be a reward for an endless struggle. And once again, the One who gave us this petition to pray has been delegated by the Father to make it happen.

The kingdom is God's forward-moving program for all of history and for all of us. It will come, with or without us. But we have the privilege of allowing the Spirit of Christ to reign in us, and when we do, it is His responsibility to give us the guidance we need for our daily decisions.

The basic will of God is that we know and love Him. Then specific guidance is given as a part of a consistent, open, willing relationship with His dwelling in us.

My friend Jane expressed the sheer delight of this assurance. "Here at last is something I don't have to find, produce or push on my own strength! I'm a daughter of King Jesus. He has a plan for my life. He found me when I was floundering and confused. He assured me

84

that I am chosen, loved and forgiven. And now when I relax, He shows me what I am to do. I prayerfully think: Will it extend the kingdom in me, others and situations? What is the Lord trying to accomplish and how can I cooperate?

"When I am unsure of what's best in complicated problems, I surrender them to the Lord, knowing He will guide my thinking when the zero hour of decision comes. He always finds a way. Sometimes it's while reading the Bible, often it's in listening prayer, and other times it's through the insight of friends. And when I miss the Lord's best for me, I'm the first to know because of an inner feeling of restlessness. Then I retrace my steps and soon discover where I went wrong. And the Lord is waiting to get me going in the right direction again."

That quality of dependent trust insulates our minds from the minimizing tactics of the neutralizer. It's a vital part of putting on the helmet of hope every morning.

Recently I had the privilege of opening the United States Senate with prayer. I flew across the country and arrived in Washington, D.C., late in the afternoon. After a quiet dinner, I settled down to go to sleep, but couldn't. I paced the floor and read a bit and tried all of the relaxation techniques. Nothing seemed to work.

Finally, around two o'clock Washington time, I began to feel sleepy, but as I began to drift off, a jolting fear flooded my mind. Suppose I went to sleep now and slept right through the time I was to give the prayer on the Senate floor! For insurance I set the hotel room alarm clock for six o'clock. Then, just to be sure, I called the hotel operator and asked, "Would you please call me at ten minutes to six? I'm afraid the alarm clock here in the room might not work." She pleasantly assured me I would have a call at 5:50 A.M.

The wake-up call came right on time. "Good morning! Welcome to Washington," the operator said. Sleepily I yawned, "Good morning, ma'am," and staggered out of bed. Then I walked to the bathroom and turned on the hottest shower that I could possibly take, hoping that would stimulate some life in my bones.

Standing in the shower with suds all over me, I suddenly heard a loud, blaring, buzzing sound. It was the alarm clock going off! And so I had to get out of the shower and turn it off. As I finished my shower, I laughed to myself, "You know, Ogilvie, you really need two alarm clocks every day—one to wake you up and another to remind you of why you're up."

I don't know about you, but I need a two-alarm reminder every hour—an alarm to go off inside to remind me to wake up to the wonderful potential of life. And I need a second ring to remind me to try to do His will in all the circumstances and challenges in which I find myself.

To pray this second petition is to hear an alarm. It's to be reminded of why we were born and that our daily goal is to live for the King of the kingdom and receive His orders for what we are to do and say as faithful and obedient disciples.

But back to that morning in Washington. After opening the Senate with prayer, I attended a luncheon sponsored by Senator Mark Hatfield and Congressman Robert McEwen for a group of Washington supporters of our television ministry. The luncheon was held in Senator Hatfield's private office in the Capitol building. I noticed that the clock on the wall had several lights on it. I was told that when a vote was to be taken on the floor of the Senate, certain lights would go on at set intervals alerting Senator Hatfield to the vote. When the lights flashed, indicating only a few minutes left to vote on an important bill, the Senator excused himself and went to the Senate floor.

After he left the room, Bob McEwen said, "Do you all understand what the Senator is about to do? He's going to cast his vote on a very important bill. We all know he's studied, prayed and thought about that vote, but now he must stand for what he believes is right."

Then, looking intently around the luncheon table, Bob said, "We all have decisions we must make. The lights are flashing and calling for us to stand and be counted as we live out our faith."

It was a moving moment of reflection about the responsibility entrusted to each of us by the Lord. But the good news is that He will be with us in those otherwise lonely times of decision. When we commit those difficult choices to Him and give Him lead time to guide our thinking, He will direct us and give us courage.

Daily Bread for Tomorrow

We claim Christ's provision of power when we pray the next petition of the Hopeful Thinkers' Prayer, "Give us this day our daily bread." The word "daily" also means "for the morrow." So the petition may also be prayed, "Give us today our bread for tomorrow." That cuts at taproot any discouragement about the future.

Our Lord gives us the assurance today that we will be able to make it through the problems of tomorrow.

Without that we can't relax and enjoy today to the fullest. He will use whatever happens.

Samuel Wilberforce prayed, "Lord, for tomorrow and its needs I do not pray: keep me, guide me, love me, Lord, just for today." But the way the Lord keeps us for today encompasses what's going to happen tomorrow. And so often in all of the pronouncements that are made about how to overcome worry by not thinking about tomorrow, we have to admit the fact that part of our concern today is about tomorrow. We can't really live today until we're assured that tomorrow is going to be all right.

When someone sent me a gift to take my wife out to dinner the pleasure it provided was not just the food and the opportunity to share a special meal together. I didn't have to worry about having enough money to carry with me to pay the bill, or putting it on a credit card and being sure that I had kept enough in my account to be able to pay the charge when it finally came through. (Did you ever have that question about charging a meal?) Because of my friend's thoughtfulness I could relax and really enjoy the occasion.

What a contrast to my first date when I was in junior high school in Kenosha, Wisconsin—I took out a pretty girl for a Coke, and she ordered a banana split! I can still feel the tension I experienced as I sat on a stool at that soda fountain, wondering how I was going to pay for her treat. I had earned enough money selling papers to buy a Coke, but not a banana split. In my embarrassment, I actually bit the old-fashioned Coke glass and spilled my drink all over the counter.

Fortunately, the clerk sensed what was happening and charged me twenty cents—the amount for two

Cokes. I returned a week later, after selling more papers, and paid for the banana split. The clerk said, "I saw your face when that girl ordered a banana split, and I thought you were in trouble. When you bit the glass, I was sure of it! And I knew you'd come back to pay the rest of the bill."

In a more profound way, Jesus, the Bread of Life, wants to feed us with His own presence today, so that we can know we have the spiritual resources for tomorrow's challenges. When He does, we are no longer preoccupied with our own needs only, but those of others. The physically and spiritually hungry of the world become our agenda. We are ready to give ourselves to care for the spiritually starving people around us and to give our money to organized efforts to get food to the physically starving around the world.

Even Before You Ask ⚓

The next petition in our prayer provides a consistent flow of forgiveness—"Forgive us our debts as we forgive our debtors." This is the only one of the petitions the Lord thought it necessary to explain, as He added, "For if you forgive men their trespasses, your heavenly Father will also forgive you. But if you do not forgive men their trespasses, neither will your Father forgive your trespasses" (Matt. 6:14–15).

From this prayer we learn that our ability to receive and realize our own forgiveness is inseparably related to our forgiving others. We become discouraged when we harbor memories of our own and others' failures, so we need a daily cleansing.

The petition for a forgiven, forgiving mind is linked

89

closely with the previous petition for bread today for the morrow, putting our prayer for forgiveness into a today-and-tomorrow perspective. It means that we need forgiveness today for past failures and assurance that we have been forgiven even before we fail in the future. That assurance eliminates the fear of the future. And the amazing thing is that we fail less when we know that we have been forgiven even before we ask.

This has a powerful effect on our relationships with others. As we experience forgiveness for our past failures, we become free to forgive all that's been done to us. And as we know we are forgiven today for tomorrow's failures, we can offer the same liberating assurance to others about what they might do in the future. This means that we no longer need to live with the fear of being let down or hurt by others because we have decided to forgive before that happens!

It's interesting, isn't it, that when we live with expectation that people will disappoint us, they usually do! However, a commitment to forgive even before people mess up really frees us of judgmentalism and liberates them to seek to please God and not us. This is a life-changing truth!

⚓ Follow the Leader

The final petition of the Hopeful Thinkers Prayer is, "Lead us not into temptation but deliver us from evil." And once again the Father delegates the risen, victorious Christ to implement this prayer in our lives. It is really a prayer of commitment to follow His leadership in our thinking.

This truth becomes clear through the second half of

the petition as we understand that the Lord has delivered us from the evil one and is with us to give us daily victory. He does that by leading us *away* from temptation to give in to the neutralizer's influence. So the prayer "Lead us not into temptation" is really claiming that the Lord is our leader and that He is able to guide our thinking away from patterns of thought that would end in actions contrary to His best for us.

Paul states our assurance vividly. "No temptation has overtaken you except such as is common to man; but God is faithful, who will not allow you to be tempted beyond what you are able, but with the temptation will also make the way of escape, that you may be able to bear it" (1 Cor. 10:13).

We can be certain that Christ will show the way by giving us clear guidance and strength. He knows how the neutralizer works and can meet him at the pass before he influences our thinking. Speaking of Christ's protective power over our minds, the author of Hebrews says, "For in that He Himself has suffered, being tempted, He is able to aid those who are tempted" (Heb. 2:18). In Greek, the word translated "aid" literally means "run to the cry." When we ask Christ to lead us, He runs to our cry for help and gives us exactly what we need.

The Beneficent Because

The doxology at the conclusion of the Hopeful Thinkers' Prayer contains what I like to call the "beneficent because." The word "for" in the phrase "for Yours is the kingdom and the power and the glory forever" really means "because" in the original Greek.

91

We can pray that God's name be hallowed, that His kingdom come and will be done, that we would be free from worry about our needs tomorrow, that we become forgiven, forgiving people, that we can claim deliverance from the evil one and guidance away from temptation—*because*—God reigns as Sovereign. He has all power and will show us His glory.

So we move from petition to praise. That's the plume on our helmet of hope, because a mind filled with praise to God has no room left for negative, restricted thinking or the neutralizer's influence.

To pray this doxology is to give our grateful response to life's three most important questions: Who is on the throne of our life? Where is our power? And who gets the glory?

Our answers as hopeful thinkers are strong and firm. We belong to the King, and His kingdom is our purpose. Our power is that we know that we are powerless without the power of the King. And our privilege is to reflect His glory in our lives. We say with Paul, "For it is God who commanded light to shine out of darkness who has shown in our hearts to give the light of the glory of God in the face of Jesus Christ. But we have this treasure in earthen vessels, that the excellence of the power may be of God and not to us!" (2 Cor. 4:6-7).

⚓ So Be It!

With our helmet of hope firmly in place, we can say "Amen, so be it." Our amen, though, is not an afterthought to conclude our prayer as hopeful thinkers, but our battle cry. It is a word of acclamation, consecration, and determination. We acclaim the Lord's love and providential care; we let go of our anxious fears, committing them to Him; and we move ahead to follow what He has guided us to do in the very problems that have discouraged us.

I have a friend who punctuates his sermons with, "Say 'Amen!' Hear?" When I heard him preach in his heavy southern drawl, I wasn't sure whether he meant "hear" or "here." He later explained that it was "hear," short for "Do you hear me?" I rather liked what I thought he meant—"Say 'Amen!' Hear?"

In whatever circumstances are ours here and now, whatever the things or people or situations that tempt us to be discouraged, we need to live our "Amen!" of complete trust. Our minds have been renewed, our thinking re-oriented, our vision rejuvenated. Our helmet of hope is on, and we can face the battle.

NOTES

1. Horatius Bonar, "Praise Him in the Heavens" (1866).

Chapter Five

THE DOOR OF HOPE

We all fail. Most every day. We make little mistakes, and sometimes larger ones. I suppose we're all haunted by the memory of what seems like a great failure to us, although with the passing of time it has probably taken on far more importance in our imagination than the original event held. To brood over a past failure and nurse its memory by thinking of "what might have been" is something we humans seem to have a compulsion to do. But that is deadly, for it cripples our ability to hope.

That was the case with Jim, an eighty-year-old man who came to talk with me about a failure he had experiences when he was just a boy of fifteen. He had never told anyone about it, and for sixty-five years he'd lived with that secret locked up inside him!

"How sad!" we say, shaking our heads with mingled sympathy and amazement. "Why did he wait so long to tell someone and get rid of that memory?" we wonder. And then we think of our own hidden failure from last week, a month ago, or a long time ago. Maybe that's why we've had such a hard time being more hopeful.

To dwell on such times, as Jim had, can rob us of our ability to be positive and hopeful. We find ourselves asking, "How can we deserve to have a bright hope for the future?"

The apostle Paul gave us the remedy, though, when he urged us to forget the past and press on to the future (Phil. 3:12-14). When we can do that, with the Lord's help, any and every past failure can be a passageway to new hope.

⚓ A Stirring Promise

That's the stirring promise God made to the people of Israel through the prophet Hosea. For forty years, from 755 B.C. to 710 B.C., during Israel's dark days, he faithfully warned of God's coming judgment of a rebellious and disobedient people. But at the same time he kept reminding them of God's forgiving love. The moving story of Hosea's marriage to Gomer, who left him to become a prostitute in pagan Baal fertility worship, enabled the prophet to identify with God's broken-hearted anguish over Israel's unfaithfulness.

With mercy and longing for things to be right again between Him and His people, God said of Israel through the prophet, "I will allure her, will bring her into the wilderness and speak comfort to her" (Hos. 2:14). In the Hebrew, the words "speak comfort to her," mean "speak to her heart." The message God wanted the people of Israel to hear was one of a new deliverance and hope. "I will give her vineyards from there, and the Valley of Achor as a door of hope; she shall sing there, as in the days of her youth, as in the day when she came up from the land of Egypt" (Hos. 2:15).

Notice the metaphor "door of hope" in that last verse. Before we can understand its full meaning, though, we need to remember what happened to Israel in the Valley of Achor. It would have been the last place the people who heard this promise would have expected to find a doorway to hope.

The Valley of Achor ⚓

For the people of Israel, the Valley of Achor was synonymous with failure. They knew the story of how their ancestors under Joshua captured the city of Jericho. The instructions then had been clear: all the spoils of the defeated city were sacred, and no one was to keep anything for himself.

But a man by the name of Achan refused to obey. He took a valuable robe, two hundred shekels of silver, and a gold bar, and hid them under his tent.

Meanwhile, not knowing about Achan's disobedience, Joshua led the army on to attack a place called Ai. That should have been an easy victory. Instead, Israel's forces were repulsed. Following on the heels of the spectacular victory over the formidable city of Jericho, it was a painful defeat for Joshua.

Why hadn't the Lord blessed him with victory? The commander knew something was amiss between the people of Israel and the Lord. Joshua put on sackcloth and ashes and prayed to the Lord to show him what was wrong.

99

It was then that Achan's sin was revealed and Achan and his family were executed for their disobedience. This judgment took place in a valley that was subsequently named the Valley of Achor (Josh. 7). The word *achor* was a technical term for the breaking of a taboo. "Therefore the name of that place has been called the Valley of Achor to this day" (Josh. 7:26).

⚓ Memory of Failure

The Valley of Achor was seared into Israel's national mind as a memory of failure. And the people who heard God's words through Hosea knew exactly what the Valley of Achor meant. For them it was a kind of code name for a terrible failure. And in the context of tender love, God's word to them was that their own period was a contemporary Valley of Achor because of their corruption and idolatry—their rejection of God.

⚓ A Door of Hope

But in spite of all that had happened, the Lord was now saying through the prophet Hosea that He would transform Israel's Valley of Achor into a door of hope.

We know the people of Hosea's time refused God's offer. The Northern Kingdom, Israel, fell, and the people were taken into exile. We are told, however, that some of the Israelites did remain faithful and continued to look ahead with expectation to that glad day when their Messiah would come.

And you and I look back and see in this story the foreshadowing of the coming of Jesus the Messiah in whose life, death, resurrection, and reigning power all

100

the Valleys of Achor can become doors of hope. We can sing in our own valley of failure when we meet Him there and go through our door of hope. Jesus is that door for us.

Christe the Door

With divine authority, Christ said, "I am the door. If anyone enters by Me, he will be saved . . . I have come that they may have life, and that they may have it more abundantly" (John 10:9, 10).

Paul describes a person who has passed through Christ, who is the door to the abundant life, as a new creation. "Therefore, if anyone is in Christ, he is a new creation; old things have passed away; behold, all things have become new. Now all things are of God, who has reconciled Himself through Jesus Christ . . ." (2 Cor. 5:17–18).

Putting those three promises together gives us a passageway out of our own Valleys of Achor. The place of our failure can be our open door of hope to the future. Authentic hope is Christ's gift of promise to us that He will do, without question, everything He said He would.

Now, it's time for a personal reality check again. Why is it so hard to appropriate these promises of hope in dealing with our big failures? With the door of hope open before us, why don't we go through it and get on with life? Let's talk about that.

Locked in a Syndrome

A primary reason for our failure to go through our door of hope is that we get locked in a syndrome. We keep going around and around in the same circle. For lots of reasons, we fail—circumstances, mistakes, poor judgment, mishaps, taking on too much, other people's goofs, or, like Achan, just plain willfulness in doing what we knew was wrong. Whatever the cause, we've got the failure staring us in the face.

But that's not all we've got: along with the failure, we've got our own self-condemnation. "How could I have been so stupid?" we say. We sabotage our own future, feeling unworthy of being hopeful. We know we need hope, but we can't seem to grasp it for ourselves.

⚓ Patricia's Plight

Patricia was locked in that syndrome. She was so down on herself because of a failure in the past that she just couldn't muster up any hope about the future. Her husband kept saying, "I wish you could be more hopeful. You're really becoming a drag." She tried hard to change, but felt blocked inside.

Before her marriage to Tom, Patricia had a secret abortion. It was one of the things she had promised herself she would never do. She had been raised by parents who were avidly against this practice.

A couple of years after her abortion, Patricia met and fell in love with Tom. His strong anti-abortion convictions made her resolve that she would never tell him her secret. But her own inner feeling of self-criticism and unworthiness churned through her mind all through the first five years of their marriage. In fact, she secretly took birth control pills in order not to become pregnant. She didn't feel worthy to be a mother.

102

Patricia knew my pro-life stance, but she had also heard me say often that I didn't want our church to be a house of judgment in which women who have had abortions could not find help in working through their feelings of failure and guilt and experiencing healing.

When Patricia came to talk with me, she mentioned Tom's comment that he wished she could be a more hopeful person. She agreed that he was probably right. We then began to explore possible reasons for her attitude. But as we talked, I began to sense that she was not being totally open with me.

Knowing the close link between failure in the past and lack of hope, I said, "Patricia, we've all failed at some time in life. Sometimes it's what we consider a really big failure, maybe even a devastating one, so we try to keep it hidden. Could that be your problem?"

Tears rolled down Patricia's face, and her body shook as she sobbed out the whole story about her abortion. After she finished, I told her about the Lord's gracious love and acceptance for her and led her through a time of healing prayer.

Then we prayed for Tom, asking the Lord to give him understanding and to encourage her as she put this memory behind her and tried to move ahead to become a hope-filled person. Before leaving she asked if I would be present when she told Tom her secret.

A few days later, when Tom and Patricia sat down in my study, I opened the conversation. "Tom, can you remember a time when you did something you considered a great failure?" He sat quietly thinking, obviously wondering where the conversation was headed. Then he nodded, "Yes, I can, why?"

"Well," I replied, "bear that in mind as Patricia tells   **103** you something that's been troubling her for a long time."

As you can imagine, that wasn't an easy, or a short, conference with Tom and Patricia. Nor was it the only one. But, in spite of this problem, the two of them had a lot going for them. They both believed in Christ, loved each other deeply, and were willing to talk and pray through this problem. At the same time, Tom had to deal with some secret failures of his own that he'd never told Patricia.

I'm happy to say that this couple made it through that difficult time. And Patricia has become a very hope-filled, positive person. She faced her private Valley of Achor and found in it a door of hope. A few days ago she and Tom had a baby girl. "Are you going to name your daughter Hope?" I asked when I called the hospital. "No," Patricia laughed, "but she's certainly a 'hope child'!"

A memory of failure no longer debilitated Patricia's ability to hope. What happened to her when she faced her failure can happen to all of us.

⚓ There's Hope for You

The other day, I visited the office of my friend Ted, a successful Chicago businessman. On his desk is a plaque engraved with the words "There's hope for you!" I asked him if there was a story behind the plaque.

Ted told me about an excruciating failure he'd gone through in his business years before. He lost everything. At what he called "bottom below bottom," Ted was forced to face his economic plight and his spiritual emptiness.

104

Some Christian businessmen who met over lunch each Thursday in the Chicago Loop took him under their wing. One of the men always ended his conversations with Ted with the parting shot, "Ted, there's hope for you!" Eventually Ted began to believe it, and one day he committed his life to Christ.

Ted told me, "I was never a very hopeful person before meeting Christ. It's been nonstop hope ever since. I keep that plaque to remind me where I was and that I'm where I am today because of the Lord. It also is a good conversation starter. Everybody needs to be told, 'There's hope for you.'"

Ted's Valley of Achor had not been some terrible sin, or even poor management, but a series of tough circumstances in the oil industry that had caused his little equipment company to go belly up. The key thing is that what *he* thought of in those dark days as dismal failure became a door of hope.

To be sure, the Lord deals with each of us differently, but we can be equally certain that He is always ready and eager to lead us out of our personal valleys of failure and plant within our hearts His own Spirit, which is the Hope of the world.

Heroes Not Exempt

When we read accounts of the lives of some of our historical heroes, we are surprised and then reassured that sometimes it took Valleys of Achor for them to go through the door of hope.

For example, Philip Melanchthon, a leading scholar in the German Reformation, was in the valley of spiritual defeat when Martin Luther wrote him a letter. **105**

"From the bottom of my heart," Luther said, "I am against those worrying cares which are taking the heart out of you. Why make God a liar in not believing His wonderful promises, when He commands us to be of good cheer, and cast all our care upon Him, for He will sustain us? Do you think He throws such words to the winds? . . . Christ has died for sin once for all, but for righteousness and truth He will not die, but live and reign. Why then worry, seeing He is at the helm? He who has been our Father will also be the Father of our children. As for me (whether it proceeds from God's Spirit or from stupidity, the Lord Jesus knows), I do not torment myself about such matters."

But, in fact, years before that letter to Melanchthon, Luther *had* tormented himself. As a monk he had flagellated himself for his spiritual failures. His Valley of Achor became a door of hope when studying Habakkuk 2:4, "But the just shall live by his faith." He took up his pen and wrote "Sola!" (the Latin word for "alone") in the margin of the text. "The just shall live by faith alone" became his battle cry.

The hope he had experienced in his personal valley enabled him to encourage his friend Melanchthon. Luther's letter may have sounded to you as if he had forgotten what he had been through himself. But the Lord has a wonderful way of helping us forget the failures that opened the way for our passage through the door of hope.

Luther and Melanchthon encouraged each other throughout the tumultuous years of the Protestant Reformation. Melanchthon's life verse became Romans 8:31, "If God is for us, who can be against us?" In his correspondence, lectures, and records of his conversations, this verse is quoted more than any other. The words of the verse are inscribed in Latin over his study door in his house in Wittenberg to this day.

A Need for Hope in Every Age

One hundred and ninety-two years after Luther's death, the reading of the introduction to his commentary on Romans by a group of Moravians had a profound effect on a thirty-six-year-old clergyman of the Church of England who was in his own valley of defeat. He had returned from a very unsuccessful missionary journey to America and was broken by his lack of spiritual power.

The clergyman wrote in his journal on May 4, 1738, "In the evening I went very unwillingly to Society in Aldersgate, where one was reading Luther's preface to the Epistle to the Romans. About a quarter before nine, while he was describing the change which God works in the heart through faith in Christ, I felt my heart strangely warmed. I felt I did trust in Christ, Christ alone for salvation; and an assurance was given me that He had taken away my sins, even mine, and saved me from the law of sin and death." Note the door of hope in the clergyman's Valley of Achor.

Filled with that hope, this man stirred England into a great revival. In the wake of that revival came social reform that changed the nation. Speaking of the Bible, from which he drew promises for a solid basis of hope, he said, "O give me that book! At any price, give me the book of God. I have it; here is enough for me!" And he preached hope from the Book's promise in over eight hundred sermons a year for fifty years, resulting in the conversion and renewal of hundreds of thousands.

The man's name was John Wesley.

Hope in the Valley of Despair

About two years before Wesley's Aldersgate experience, the Lord opened the door of hope for a man at Oxford by the name of George Whitefield.

Whitefield was in a valley of despair. He had tried to change his own life by seeking to be more spiritual. He denied himself every luxury, wore old ragged clothes, fasted and gave away all he had, longing to know Christ personally. But nothing worked. There was something wrong at the core of his being.

One day he read Henry Scougal's *The Life of God in the Soul of Man*. It gave him hope. For the first time he discovered the secret of Christ's being formed within him as the hope of glory (Col. 1:27). Whitefield said, "When I read this, a ray of divine light instantaneously darted upon my soul; and, from that moment, but not till then, did I know that I must become a new creature . . . And oh! With what joy unspeakable and full of glory—was I filled, when the weight of sin left me and an abiding sense of the pardoning love of God broke upon my disconsolate soul!"

He then told his friends and family, "I have found that there is such a thing as the new birth!" One central message, "You must be born again," was the theme he preached with amazing results all over Great Britain and America until he died in 1770.

Looking back on his experience of hope in his Valley of Achor, he said, "I know the exact place. It may perhaps be superstitious, but, whenever I go to Oxford, I cannot help running to the spot where Jesus Christ first revealed Himself to me and gave me a new birth."

Reading the biographies and autobiographies of people the Lord has used throughout Christian history is one of my favorite hobbies. And I'm constantly impressed with the fact that it was usually in some valley of failure and defeat, some spiritual emptiness or powerlessness that they passed through their door of hope. But there's another common thread in the stories of our spiritual ancestors. There were repeated valleys of need in which they experienced fresh hope.

It's no less true for us. After the Lord has helped us overcome some new failure or defeat, He gives us another opportunity to express our renewed hope.

The Door of Opportunity ⚓

We soon discover that the door of hope becomes a door of opportunity. In the New Testament the metaphor of the door is used for Christ, and also for new challenges.

It was after Paul went through the painful experience of a broken relationship with Mark on the first missionary journey that he experienced his first success in reaching the Gentiles for Christ. Note the use of the word "door" in Acts 14:27. Paul and Barnabas "reported all that God had done with them, and that He had *opened the door of faith* to the Gentiles" (italics added).

During his second missionary journey, Paul again went through a difficult time before moving through the next door of opportunity. The apostle was convinced that the Roman province of Asia was the next **109** step in the strategy of reaching the Gentile world. And undoubtedly he had in mind preaching Christ in Ephesus, the great stronghold of pagan worship in the Temple of Diana.

But it was not to be. Ephesus was on the Lord's agenda for a later time. Luke tells us in Acts 16:6 that Paul was "forbidden by the Holy Spirit to preach the word in Asia." That door was closed. Then when Paul approached the borders of Mysia and wanted to go northeast into Bithynia, that door was closed too. Somewhat confused about where the Lord was trying to lead him, Paul headed for Troas on the Aegean coast.

Paul's struggle in his valley of indecision had been perplexing. But the Lord knew what He was doing. At Troas, He opened a door of hope and opportunity for the next big campaign of spreading the gospel to Greece.

In a similar way, we go through times when we feel blocked in getting on with what we think is best for us. We get frustrated when things don't work out the way we've planned. Sometimes we even blunder ahead in directions the Lord has not guided, or has clearly shown us are not His intended plan for us. Finally, when things obviously aren't working, we cry out to the Lord, telling Him that, at long last, we are ready to do things His way. That's when He sets before us a new door of hope and opportunity.

⚓ Open Doors Leading to People

110 Most often, the Lord's door of hope and opportunity leads to people He has prepared to receive His

love. That was the case for Paul with the church at Philadelphia. When Paul was finally guided to go to the province of Roman Asia and preach for a prolonged period in Ephesus, the gospel spread to the key cities of the area. One of those was Philadelphia, located on a Roman road that was the main trade route through the province. Thousands of travelers passed through the city each year. The Christians there needed to realize the strategic door of opportunity the Lord had given them to share the gospel with the constantly changing procession of potential converts.

Christ communicated His vision for the Philadelphian Christians' untapped potential in a challenge he communicated through the apostle John. "These things says He who is holy, He who is true, 'He who has the key of David, He who opens and no one shuts, and shuts and no one opens': I know your works. See, I have set before you an open door, and no one can shut it; for you have a little strength, have kept My word, and have not denied My name" (Rev. 3:7–8).

Our Door of Opportunity

The same open door of opportunity stands before you and me. Wherever the Lord has placed us is a strategic place to communicate hope to people. That's the special calling of those who have experienced hope in their own Valley of Achor. Nothing is wasted, not even our failures. They bring us to the Lord and put us in touch with people.

The point is—most of the people around us are living in some valley of memory of failure. They

111

desperately need the hope we've received in our own valley. They are presenting us with an open door through which we can go and love by sharing our hope.

In fact, if we're not actively involved in the ministry of spreading hope, we are displaying a sure sign that we are still in our Valley of Achor with our own brand of Achor's sin. To hide the treasure of the gospel under our tents and act as if it is our private possession—that, perhaps, is the greatest failure of all!

⚓ An Open Door

And the Lord is always ready to turn that Valley of Achor into a door of hope. The apostle John's vision of heaven also communicates to us the changeless nature of our Lord. "After these things I looked, and behold, a door standing open in heaven" (Rev. 4:1). That door will never be closed to you and me. It will always be a door of hope for us and a door of opportunity for sharing that hope with others.

Listen as John Masefield vividly portrays the double door of hope and opportunity.

> And God who gives beginning gives the end.
> . . . .
> A rest for broken things too broke to mend.[1]

And then:

> The bolted door had broken in,
> I knew that I was done with sin.
> I knew that Christ had given me birth
> To brother all the souls on earth. . . .[2]

NOTES

1. John Masefield, *The Widow in the Bye Street,* in *The Everlasting Mercy* and *The Widow in the Bye Street* (New York: Macmillan, 1916; copyright 1911 by John Masefield), p. 221.

2. John Masefield, *The Everlasting Mercy* (New York: Macmillan, 1916; copyright 1912 by The Macmillan Company), p. 78.

Chapter Six

Chapter Six

HOPE
IN
HARD
TIMES

She asked an honest question that deserved an honest answer.

"How can you be so hopeful after all you've been through?" The questioner was referring to my fall at the Scotland coast when my leg was so badly broken and my very life had been in danger.

"I'm more hopeful now *because* of what I've been through," I responded. That led into a long conversation about how hope can be deepened by the difficulties of life.

Life either makes us hard or more hopeful. For some people, the difficulties of life drive them further into hopelessness. For others, the difficulties become opportunities for hope to become more vital. The great difference is whether Hope Himself lives in us.

So far we've talked about hope as the indwelling   **117**

Spirit of Christ and that we become hopeful thinkers when He takes up residence in our minds.

But we are not inanimate, mechanical containers of His Spirit. We are human beings capable of immense growth as hopeful people. When Christ establishes a beachhead in our minds, He then wants to transform our total nature until we are like Him. Often, it's in the trials of life that this takes place.

⚓ The Vale of Soul Making

In the winter of 1819, John Keats wrote George and Georgiana Keats some lines I've quoted often. They have taken on new meaning for me during this past year since my accident. Keats wrote, "Nothing ever becomes real until you have experienced it—even a proverb is no proverb to you until your life has illustrated it. Call the world, if you please, 'The vale of soul making.'"[1]

It's in the vale of difficulties that Christ enables our souls—our inner life—to grow. Truths we've professed begin to possess us. We *become* the convictions we have held theoretically. A bridge is built between our talk and our walk in the Christian life. Life is intended to give us depth of personality in which surface beliefs become the fabric of our character.

⚓ Hope in Weakness

And it's often in our weakness that Christ makes us spiritually strong. That's been difficult for me to learn. Before my accident, I had tried to appear to be strong. When I hobbled back into the chancel of my church to lead worship, it was difficult to preach leaning heavily on a cane. As I struggled up and down the steps, people sat watching anxiously, afraid I would fall. The long convalescence had left me physically drained. Pain was written on my face. I was weak and everyone knew it. But I knew something else. In my weakness, Christ was making me spiritually stronger than ever before.

I'm thankful that hope surged through my weakness. It put me in touch with people who also were suffering and in all kinds of pain. And those who were pretending to be strong were given permission to admit their weakness and grow in hope. It's been a great time of renewal for me and for our church.

Now as I write this a year after my accident, and look back on all I learned, I pray that I'll never forget that Christ uses us just as we are. When we can't rely on human strength and skill, He shines through us in a powerful way. And the glory goes to Him and not to us.

The Lord is growing a soul and building a hopeful character in us, and it's so obviously His miracle that people give Him the praise and want the same hope for their own lives.

Growing a Character

The apostle Paul gives us a vivid description of how the Lord enables us to grow a hopeful character. In his letter to the Christians at Rome, he shows us how hope is deepened in the tribulations of life. I'm going to quote the passage in its entirety so we can have it at hand, and then we can digest in bite-sized portions the progressive steps Paul gives us for growth in experiencing greater hope.

⚓ Peace, Joy, and Hope

Note how Paul goes from peace to joy and then on to hope in this encouraging passage.

> Therefore, having been justified by faith, we have peace with God through our Lord Jesus Christ, through whom also we have access by faith into this grace in which we stand, and rejoice in hope of the glory of God. And not only that, but we also glory in tribulations, knowing that tribulation produces perseverance; and perseverance, character; *and character, hope. Now hope does not disappoint,* because the love of God has been poured out in our hearts by the Holy Spirit who was given to us (Rom. 5:1–5, italics added).

Paul is telling us in those electric words that because of our faith in what God has done for us in Christ we know with assurance that we are loved. As we've stressed in previous chapters, it is out of this that confident hope is born. The grace, unqualified acceptance, of Christ is the object of our own experience of hope. And the focus of that hope is, as Paul puts it, the glory of God.

To Paul, the glory of God means being made in the likeness of Christ. He makes this clear in writing to the Christians at Corinth:

> Now the Lord is the Spirit, and where the Spirit of the Lord is, there is liberty. But we all, with unveiled face, beholding as in a mirror the glory of the Lord, are being transformed into the same image from glory to glory, just as by the Spirit of the Lord. . . . For we do not preach ourselves, but Christ Jesus the Lord,

and ourselves your servants for Jesus' sake. For it is God who commanded light to shine out of darkness who has shone in our hearts to give the light of the knowledge of the glory of God in the face of Jesus Christ (2 Cor 3:17-18; 4:5-6).

Centering our attention on Christ, receiving His Spirit, begins the process of transformation into His likeness. The glory of God is a woman or man fully alive in His Son. He has called us and justified us so He could glorify us in Christ (Rom. 8:30). That's our fulfilled, yet to be consummated, hope. It takes a lifetime.

Next, going back to his words in chapter 5 of Romans, Paul writes, "We glory in tribulation" (v. 3). Really? How can that be?

Mollified by Tribulation ⚓

I believe the heart of what Paul is saying here is that our inner life is like clay. Tribulation can either harden or mollify, that is, soften, that clay. If we are willing, it will soften us. And it is then that the Lord, the divine Potter of our characters and personalities, can put us on the wheel for reshaping.

What He said to Israel during a particularly difficult time of tribulation, He says to us, "Look, as the clay is in the potter's hand, so are you in My hand, O house of Israel!" (Jer. 18:6).

The Greek word for tribulation is *thlipsis*, meaning a pressing, or pressure. It is used for whatever happens to us that burdens our spirits. In street language, tribulation is whatever gets us down—on ourselves, others, life. It may be the pressure of problems, mental anguish, physical pain, antagonism of people, or rejection and persecution because of our convictions.

Paul used the word tribulation in reference to the rejection and persecution he had endured himself and to the persecution the Christians at Rome were facing. But in a positive sense, tribulation or difficulties can be whatever brings us to cry out for the Lord's help and causes us to grow in Him.

My friends Niko and Ellen Smith know what that means. Niko is the white pastor of the all-black parish church in the all-black township of Mamelodi, on the outskirts of Pretoria, South Africa. He and Ellen, who is a doctor, are the only white residents in the township. As a native Afrikaner and clergyman of the Dutch Reformed Church, Niko's acceptance of a call to a black church not only put into action his strong opposition to apartheid, but caused him to be rejected by the established church. He has suffered ridicule and threats on his life. Telephone calls in the night remind Niko and Ellen of the danger. "Now that you're living with the kaffers," whites say, "when we come to shoot them, we'll shoot you too." But the Smiths continue preaching the gospel and serving the immense needs of the people of Mamelodi.

In 1961, when Niko was still in the established church, Karl Barth asked him, "Are you free to preach the truths of the gospel in South Africa?" Niko could not answer the question truthfully then, but he can now. He is a free man in Christ who, at high risk, is living what he believes.

When Niko preached in our church in Hollywood, he shared with me how he had to trust the Lord to sustain him more than ever before in his life. He's soft clay in the Potter's hand and, having visited with him several times in recent years, I can see the magnificent person God is shaping.

In a different way, some of the members of our church who are in the movie business have put their careers on the line when they have refused to take parts or participate in the production of films that compromised their beliefs.

Even as I'm writing now, our Hollywood congregation is taking a firm stand against Universal Pictures' production and release of Martin Scorcese's film of Nikos Kazantzakis' novel, *The Last Temptation of Christ*. This film portrays Jesus as a vacillating, confused, hallucinating, sex-distressed carpenter who, prior to His ministry, makes crosses for the execution of fellow Jews. Jesus' ministry is characterized, with too few exceptions, more by the haunting pursuit of Satan than an assurance that He is the divine Son of God filled with the power of God. And during the crucifixion, Christ is portrayed as having a fantasy in which He marries Mary Magdalene and later has children by both Martha and Mary of Bethany.

We had to speak out against this film. Many of our church members in the media are standing up to be counted against this blasphemy against their Savior. Some of them are finding their witness very costly at work and among their friends.

Taking a stand for what we believe is required wherever we live or work. There are soul-sized issues facing your city, just as there are in mine. Sometimes opposition comes from the people closest to us. It causes trouble, pressure to change our convictions or face rejection.

So tribulation can be personal in our own needs or social as a result of the way we feel led to live out our faith in our relationships and responsibilities. We all have our own set of problems and difficulties.

The question is: Are we rejoicing in them, thanking the Lord that they have softened our hard inner core and made us willing clay on the Potter's wheel? Do we trust Him?

⚓ Molded by Patient Perseverance

When we feel the hands of the Potter on our softened clay, we are given patient perseverance. "Tribulation produces perseverance," says Paul. The Greek word for perseverance is *hupomone*, meaning "remaining under." It is often translated as patience or endurance.

We are able to remain under the Potter's hand because we know how much God loves us. He did not cause our difficulties, but He certainly knows how to use them to shape us into the people He has planned for us to become. "I will not forget you," He says. "See, I have inscribed you on the palms of My hands" (Isa. 49:15–16).

Paul reminded the Christians in Ephesus of this endurance-building assurance when he wrote, "For we are His workmanship created in Christ Jesus for good works, which God prepared beforehand that we should walk in them" (Eph. 2:10). I'm always renewed in my patience when I remember that the Greek word for "workmanship" is *poiema*, denoting "something that is made," often referring to a thing of beauty and perfection. Our English word "poem" comes from this

124

Greek word. A poem has flow, symmetry, order, balance.

God, through His ever-present hand in Christ, is up to great things in our lives. He's shaping a beautiful person inside us, working out the lumps in the clay, the quirks of personality and the debilitating attitudes that could keep us from the realization of our full potential.

Patience is a special quality the Lord kneads into us. It is one of the fruits of the Spirit, the code name Paul used for the spiritual "transplant" that takes place when the nature of Christ is formed in us and begins to grow.

I've come to believe that our problem with impatience is that we misunderstand patience. It is not acquiescence, or perpetual placidity, or lack of fiber. Patience must be rooted in the overriding confidence that God is in control of this universe, our world, and our lives. We need to know that God does work things together for good for those who love Him. A patient person knows the shortness of time and the length of eternity. Patience is really faith in action. No wonder it's one of the fruit of the Spirit. It is one of the matchless characteristics of Christ Himself.

If we would learn patience, the Lord alone can teach us. There are many facsimiles of the quality, but authentic patience comes as a result of a deep personal relationship with Christ. He gives us courage to endure and not give up.

Media magnate Walter Annenberg said, "There are two great sources of inspiration in life, enthusiasm and tragedy. And I have been boxed in by both. But having been boxed in by both, I also recognize that perseverance is the key to escape and satisfaction."

125

⚓ **An Experienced Encourager**

My friend Al Bush of Tulsa, Oklahoma, has experienced the power of perseverance. He has been one of the Lord's special encouragers for me this past year. He knows what it's like to trust the Lord for endurance.

Some years ago while Al was in Los Angeles on business, the car he was driving was hit broadside on the driver's side by a massive truck moving at high speed. His whole left side was crushed, and he also suffered eight compound fractures. When he came to in the hospital, he heard the surgeons discussing the possible amputation of one of his legs. Al's wife, Marilyn, pleaded with them not to do that, but to find some way to save it. Finally they repaired the leg by putting steel plates above and below the knee. They set his other broken bones and put him in a body cast. He was in traction for five months. Eventually he was sent home to Tulsa.

It was not easy for Al to wait for the long period of healing. He's an active, dynamic businessman, a champion handball player and an energetic jogger, golfer, and sportsman.

For Al the endurance battle had only begun. Moment by moment, he prayed for strength and courage. After a long time, he learned to walk on crutches. He remembers slipping on the ice one morning and having to pull himself over to a building and edge himself up inch by inch. "The only thing that was hurt was my pride," he told me. He kept pressing on, unwilling to give in to discouragement.

Today Al is back at full steam as president of his own

company, active in his community, and a very highly

valued leader on the board of directors of my radio and television ministry. During my own recovery, he called frequently to say, "Lloyd, I made it and so can you!" Al is a positive encourager of endurance in others because of his own proven first-hand experiences of the Lord's faithfulness.

Now, take a moment to think back to the times in your life when the Lord gave you patient, enduring perseverance in some trial. In those times you probably discovered two things—how much He loved you and how much you love and need Him. Because of His goodness, you came through the tough time more sure of His faithfulness and more confident that your faith really works. In a sense, both the Lord and you were put to a test in your life. Now as you look back, you realize that He intervened and worked things out for your growth and His glory. And you have living proof from your own experience.

My friend Lynn knows this. She has gone through great difficulties and yet looks back with assurance. Here's how she puts it, "My hope gains momentum with each experience of the Lord's faithfulness. I am confident without doubt that there is nothing that could happen to me that could separate me from Him. He has taken me too far to let go now."

Matured in Character ⚓

That's what Paul means when he says that perseverance produces character. The Greek word he used that's translated as "character" in the New King James Version means "proven experience that is worthy of approval." In other words, it's an experience in a trial   **127** that strengthens our confidence in the Lord and assures us that we belong to Him.

An accumulation of those positive experiences builds up our character with hope. On the basis of what we've experienced in the past, we are exhilarated with hope for the future. This quality of hope does not fade. It's not crossed-fingered wishing; it is the gift of the Potter, and He's not finished with us yet.

Often we hear and use expressions like, "What a character!" or "The most unforgettable character I've ever met," or "He's got good character references." We use the word character for the composite of the qualities of people. And one of the most dynamic qualities of our character is meant to be hope.

⚓ A Twist of Insight

Now here's a twist of insight. The progression from tribulation to perseverance to character to hope also works in reverse. Hope produces character that perseveres in future difficulties. There's a two-way ebb and flow between the hope the Lord develops in us through trials and the matured hope we express in confronting the problems around us in people and society.

German writer and churchman Jürgen Moltmann said, "Those who hope in Christ can no longer put up with reality as it is, but begin to suffer under it, to contradict it. Peace with God means conflict with the world, for the goods of the promised future stab inexorably into the flesh of any unfulfilled present."

There is no emeritus status for people in whom the Lord is molding a hopeful character. We are never retired to an honorary position with no responsibilities.

Hope presses us on to ask and answer some crucial questions that define His next steps for our growth:

- In what ways do I need to grow in Christlikeness?
- Where is the Potter seeking to place His hand on the clay of my character?
- Who in my life needs hope? To whom am I called to communicate unqualified love and unreserved forgiveness?
- Are any of my relationships taut, frayed or broken? What is my hope for reconciliation?
- What are the Lord's next steps for the deepening of my marriage or friendships? If I threw caution to the wind, what would the Lord have me do about it?
- If the Lord had His way with my church, what needs reformation and renewal? What is the boldest hope the Lord has given me for the church in America? My own local church?
- Which one of the major social problems of my community am I called to confront and become involved in solving with the Lord's guidance and courage?

We can never stop asking these questions as long as we live. Some of them, especially the ones about our churches and our society, may lead into conflict and trying times. But just as our hope has been nurtured in trials in the past, it will grow even more in the new challenges the Lord proposes. Hopeful people are not "wrestless"—without struggles—but restless. Of course, we rest in the Lord to renew our strength and vision, but that's rest in preparation for the next advance in the battle.

129

My wife, Mary Jane, has a butcher who answers her question, "Well, how are you?" with a jaunty "Almost perfect!" The other day, she asked, "What would it take to make you perfect?" He just went on cutting the meat; he didn't answer the question.

In the New Testament the word "perfect" means possessing maturity, completeness, reaching the goal that has been set. And the Lord constantly moves the goal, just when we think we've arrived at the finish line. He gives us a second wind, the breath of His own Spirit, to run on with the fresh oxygen of hope. Emil Brunner was right: What oxygen is to the lungs, hope is to the soul.

But, let's face it, there are times, when the goal line is moved further away to encourage us to press on, that we'd like to drop out of the race. We all have times when we realize that moving on to reach the mandates of the Master will stretch us and we're not sure we are willing. That forces us to answer the Lord's question to Israel, "Shall the clay say to him who forms it, 'What are you making?'" (Isa. 45:9). Sometimes our honest answer would be, "Well, Lord, I guess I do wonder at times. As a matter of fact, I'd like to have things remain as they are for awhile."

That's a sure sign that we need a fresh experience of hope—a backward look, then an inward look, then an upward look and then finally a forward look.

We need to remember how the Lord has given us hope in hard times. Looking inward, we can see the progress He has accomplished in making us hopeful characters during those times. Then we can look to Him and pray, "Lord, I know you are not finished with me. You always have hope for me. Now give me

130

renewed hope for myself and get me moving again. You are the Potter and I am Your clay." I've never prayed that prayer without being given a new forward look and hope.

And what do we see out ahead of us? Christ, calling us on to new challenges, yes. But those challenges are also opportunities to grow in hope in the "vale of soul making." The Lord will not leave or forsake us. The trials of the past have proven that to us. And if we fail Him, He'll use even those times to lead us into greater hope. And so we pray with Robert Browning:

> So take and use Thy work:
> Amend the flaws that lurk.
> What strain of the stuff,
> What warpings past the aim!
> My times be in Thy hand!
> Perfect the cup as planned![2]

NOTES

1. John Keats, *Letters*, to George and Georgiana Keats, 14 February–3 May 1819, in *Oxford Dictionary of Quotations*, 3d ed. (New York: Oxford University Press, 1979), 294.

2. *Rabbi ben Ezra, Ib.* xxxii

Chapter Seven

THE
ANCHOR
OF
HOPE

Some years ago, my family and I rented a houseboat in Toms River, New Jersey. We sailed it up the Atlantic coast, through the New York Harbor, and on up the inland waterway to Sorel, Quebec. Since we were rather inexperienced sailors, we tried to spend the nights in marinas along the way. Every so often, however, we had to anchor offshore.

One evening on the St. Lawrence Seaway the water was calm and as flat as a mirror. So we decided to drop anchor in a little bay off the rocky coast.

I threw out the anchor, secured it to the bottom, and let out what I thought was an adequate amount of anchor line for a peaceful night's anchorage. The scope, or length of an anchor line, should be the ratio of about ten feet of line to each foot of distance from the anchor on the bottom of the water to the top of **135** the bow of the boat. But because everything was so tranquil, I let out a ratio of only five to one.

⚓ Panic in the Night

After a lovely dinner together on the stern of our houseboat, we all crawled into our sleeping bags for a pleasant night's rest. In the middle of the night, I was awakened by frightened shouts. From the bow of the boat, my wife Mary Jane cried, "Lloyd! Wake up! The anchor's come loose and we're heading straight into the rocks!"

I leaped out of my sleeping bag and ran to the bow. There stood Mary Jane, her nightgown flapping in the wind, holding a limp anchor line in her hand. The anchor had come loose! What I hadn't allowed for was that during the night gigantic tankers moved through the seaway, sending great swells crashing to the shore. Swells from a tanker had bounced our boat like a cork in the seaway, pulling our anchor right off the bottom. Fortunately, Mary Jane had been awakened.

Realizing our plight, I started the engine, put it in reverse, and barely avoided crashing into the shore. When I re-anchored, you can be sure I let out enough anchor line to ride out the swells.

⚓ Parables from the Sea

Over the years, as both a sailor and passenger on large and small crafts, I have been fascinated by the similarities of seamanship to sailing the ship of life. And when it comes to anchors and anchoring, the parables become very pointed.

For example, what Elliot Maloney has to say about anchoring in his book on seamanship, *Piloting*, is very applicable to our spiritual lives.

> In quiet anchorages in familiar surroundings, ground tackle (the anchor and the anchor line) and the methods used are seldom put to the test. Cruise in strange waters, with inadequate shelter in an exposed anchorage during a hard blow, and the elements will surely take the measure of both the tackle and technique. The ultimate test, of course, would come in deep water on a lee shore with nothing between you and the breakers on the beach except dependable gear. Ask yourself now, in a situation like that, would you hold or hope?
>
> The problem, then, breaks down into two principal parts—(1) the equipment we should carry, and (2) knowledge of how to use it. It is in that sequence that we must treat the subject of anchors and anchorages, however anxious we may be to plunge headlong into the "how" aspect before we are quite familiar with the "what."[1]

Taking the "what" before the "how" is the sequence I'd like to follow now as we take a close look at the most important anchor for the ship of our lives and the way it contributes to our hope.

The author of Hebrews calls it "the anchor of the soul." And he tells us both what it is and what it does for us. "This hope we have as an anchor of the soul, both sure and steadfast, and which enters the Presence behind the veil, where the forerunner has entered for us, even Jesus, having become High Priest forever according to the order of Melchizedek" (Heb. 6:19–20). **137**

The rich metaphors of this sentence provide us an impelling progression of thought about an anchor that gives us hope for the storms of life. In the fierce winds of adversity and the turbulent waves of doubt, we can have a sure and steadfast anchor that holds, a safe anchorage that's secure, and an anchor line that will not break.

Now, before we talk about these three certainties, let's take a brief personal inventory and ask ourselves, "Do I have a strong anchor on board? Do I know how to use it? Have I found a secure anchorage in which to drop that anchor? Is my anchor line firmly attached not only to the anchor but also to my life?"

⚓ Our Anchor

Take a good look at your anchor. Be very sure what kind it is. Again, the analogy of ships' anchors is helpful. On most boats there are three kinds of anchors. There is the lunch anchor. It is small, lightweight, and used in a dinghy or for anchoring briefly in very calm waters. Then there is the working anchor, fitted to the size of the boat and used under normal circumstances. But also, most crafts have onboard what is called a storm anchor. This anchor is heavier and stronger and is kept for emergencies in very turbulent weather.

It seems to me the storm anchor is the one we need on our life-craft. It is an anchor for all seasons—one that works in the squalls of unexpected difficulties and holds when we must ride out the prolonged blows and blasts of life's relentless problems. But in order to realize the worth of the anchor, we need to feel the stress of the storm.

Hope is our storm anchor. "This hope we have as an anchor of the soul," says the author of Hebrews. He has explained the distinctive power of that hope throughout the sixth chapter of his epistle. Using the example of God's faithfulness to Abraham, he reminds us that our God is a God who makes and keeps His promises. We can stake our lives on His unchanging plan and purpose and His promise to be with us.

God's purpose for us and all creation is focused in Christ. His plan is that you and I should experience His judgment and reconciling love in Christ. His promise is that we can take an honest look at our lives and receive power to dare to be different. This is the hope the author of Hebrews is talking about.

So our central theme is that real hope is not a frail feeling of anxious anticipation, but is the Spirit of the Living Christ. We cannot place hope in Him unless He first infuses it in us. He is the anchor of our lives. And that anchor has a very special quality, as we shall see.

A Sure and Steadfast Anchor

Christ our hope is an anchor that is "both sure and steadfast." These words describe an anchor that is made of strong, tough, tempered iron. It can take whatever strain is placed on it. There is no danger of its shank breaking or its flukes being dislodged. It digs in and gets a solid hold; it will not drag when the sea is rough or the gale winds blow. A "sure and steadfast" anchor is dependable, safe, and worthy of trust. And that's the kind of anchor of hope Christ is for us.

139

⚓ **An Awesome Anchorage**

Now let's turn our attention to the awesome anchorage where Christ anchors our souls. To do that we must follow the train of thought of the author of Hebrews in the verses we introduced earlier in this chapter. Note how he shifts his metaphors from nautical language to the architecture of the temple in Jerusalem. "This hope we have as an anchor of the soul, both sure and steadfast, and which enters the Presence behind the veil where the forerunner has entered for us, even Jesus . . ." (Heb. 6:19–20)

Inside the Temple, beyond the Court of the Women and the Court of the Men, was the Holy Place. Beyond that was the Holy of Holies, an area separated from the Holy Place by a thickly woven, heavy veil. Behind the veil in the Holy of Holies was the Ark of the Covenant, containing the tablets of stone on which the Ten Commandments were carved. Over the Ark of the Covenant was a covering called the Mercy Covering. It was in the Holy of Holies that the ancient Hebrews believed that the presence of Yahweh, God, dwelled.

Once a year on the great Day of Atonement, the high priest would sacrifice a lamb on the altar in the court just outside the Holy Place. Then he would take the blood into the Holy of Holies and offer it to God for the sins of the people. No one else had access to this most sacred place.

With that background, we can begin to see the powerful imagery used by the author of Hebrews. His reference to the "Presence behind the veil" is to God and the Holy of Holies.

You will remember that the veil that had separated the Holy of Holies was torn in two when Jesus died on the cross. He is not only the forerunner who has shown us the way; He has opened the way for us.

Now the imagery of the "anchor" and the "Presence" begins to make wonderful sense. Christ anchors us in the very heart of God, our Father. His heart is filled with righteousness and mercy. We are confronted with the absolute demand of the Father's commandments and are comforted with the absolute mercy of His forgiveness.

Dr. J. B. Phillips translates the promise from Hebrews as, "This hope we have as an utterly reliable anchor for our souls, fixed in the inner most shrine of heaven, where Jesus has already entered on our behalf."

Having our lives anchored in the holiness of God brings stability and strength. The Ten Commandments have not gone out of style. God still demands that we have no other gods before Him. He still requires reverence, integrity, moral purity, and accountability to Him in our relationships and responsibilities. He still condemns our envy and lust, our pride and self-centeredness. And He still calls us to be holy people, who belong to Him and live for His glory. Everything is not relative, as the New Age people try to tell us. There is only one way to live. God's way. And He has left no doubt about what He requires.

Now we must ask a tough question. With an anchor and an anchorage like that, why do we drift when the winds of problems blow and the waves of difficulty heave around us? The answer for many people is that though we believe in the anchor and the anchorage, our lives are not being held firmly with a strong anchor **141**

line. The anchor may have come loose from the ship of
our lives.

⚓ The Bitter End

The end of an anchor line secured to a ship is called
the "bitter end." It must be laced through the chocks
on the deck, down into the hull, and tied to the mast.
There is nothing worse than to have the ship's end of
the anchor line come loose so that both anchor and
anchor line are lost in the sea. No wonder the ship's
end of the anchor line is called the "bitter end."

Picture the panic you would feel if you were at anchor during a storm and suddenly you saw the "bitter
end" slipping across the deck, through the chocks, and
down the side of the hull into the sea! That's exactly
the way many people today are feeling about their day-
to-day existence. The storms of life are raging; they
know the anchor is secure; but they are not connected
to it!

⚓ Our Anchor Line

Our anchor line is an integral part of our spiritual
anchoring equipment. It keeps us firmly connected to
Christ our anchor who is lodged solidly in the anchorage of the holy heart of God. When the winds blow on
the ship of our lives, there's a tug on the anchor line,
and we know we are secure.

Spiritually, these tugs on the anchor line remind us
that we are accountable to God. Christ not only anchors
us in God's righteousness, but consistently tugs on the
142   anchor line with creative judgment of our lives. His

concern is that we not drift away from the anchorage. He consistently checks us, offering us a better way so that our final accounting and examination before God is not a bitter end. Christ's tug on the anchor line is part of His assignment to help us live now in a way that prepares us to pass the examination with flying colors.

I had three professors in my postgraduate training who gave very different kinds of examinations. One tried to trick us. He seemed to have the ability to come up with an obscure question that would expose some aspect of the material that we hadn't really learned.

Another gave no examination at all. On the surface that might seem good, but in reality it was very frustrating—a little like a courtroom without a judge, when you want to prove something. There was no closure, no way that we could say we had really learned the material. He was so easygoing that his acceptance made us feel unaccepted.

And then I had a wonderful professor who told us in advance of the examination what the questions were going to be. Preparing for the exam was a delight. I could sit down with the ten or fifteen questions and prepare myself. It would occur to me after the exam that he had selected exactly those questions that really covered all of the material. If I could answer them, I really had learned what he wanted me to get out of the course. That's the way Jesus gets us ready for our final accounting.

The Judgment of Christ ⚓

When in the Apostles' Creed we say the words "He shall come to judge the quick and the dead," we affirm the biblical belief that we are accountable to the living Christ each day of our lives. When Christ arose from the dead and ascended into heaven, God turned over to Him not only all power but also the authority to judge. The wonderful thing is that He's given us the examination questions before the examination. He's told us what the judgment's going to be and wants to get us ready. We can be prepared. When we feel His tug on the anchor line, we are reminded that we answer to Him. That's demanding, but it also makes us sure and hopeful.

⚓ ## Creative Confession

An important discovery I've made in my own relationship with Jesus Christ has been through a fresh understanding of the word "confession." The Greek word for "confession" is *homologeō*, which means to "say the same after, to agree with, to admit."

Creative confession takes place in an intimate relationship with Christ in which He helps us see the things that we need to confess. He shows us those things that are standing between us and Him, between us and any other person, and between us and our effectiveness for Him. We belong to Him and are accountable to Him. And out of His love for us, He tugs on our anchor line as needed.

⚓ ## The Ultimate Issue

The ultimate issue of our lives is our response to God's love and His forgiveness in Christ. The only response that will qualify us to live forever with Him is

144

that we believe in Christ as the Lord and the Savior of our lives.

"Oh, I'm home free," you say. "I made that declaration when I was a kid in confirmation." Others will remember making their confession of faith as an adult in worship at church, or at a conference, or with a friend, or alone in prayer. But what Christ wants to know is what's happened since. What are the actions, attitudes, habit patterns, relationships, possessions, or whatever that may have come into our lives since and that compete with our loyalty to Him? It is possible, you know, to glibly say the words of faith without a profound, intimate relationship with Him.

On Whose Strength? ⚓

But, let's move on to those wonderful words of Jesus when He says, "I am the vine, you are the branches. He who abides in Me, and I in him, bears much fruit; for without Me you can do nothing" (John 15:5). As I reflect on those words, I can picture Christ tugging at the anchor line asking this question—"Is there anything you're attempting on your own strength? Are you trying to live the Christian life on your own power? Are you out of steam, burned out, tired?"

To be in Christ is to allow Him to live in us, day by day. Is that the reality of our lives? Are we constantly being renewed by the Spirit of the living Christ in us? Do we have His fire, vision and hope? Is there evidence of the fruit of His Spirit in us—love, joy, peace, patience, kindness, goodness, faithfulness, gentleness, self-control?

Jesus says, "Not everyone who says to Me, 'Lord,   145

Lord,' shall enter the kingdom of heaven, but he who does the will of My Father in heaven" (Matt. 7:21). The will of the Father is that we become like His Son. We were never meant to attempt that alone. But some of us try. The tug on the anchor line reminds us that we can't make it alone and that Christ is ready to help us now and in the future.

⚓ ## The New Commandment

Or consider Jesus' new commandment, to love as He's loved us. "This is My commandment, that you love one another as I have loved you. Greater love has no one than this, than to lay down one's life for his friends" (John 15:12–13). Suddenly before us are all those relationships where that quality of love is absent. His love for us is an unmotivated love; He loves us because He is love, not because we deserve it.

So often we wait for other people to do and say those things that will draw out of us the measure of love we think they have earned. And Jesus was very decisive about forgiveness as an expression of love. On our day of judgment He's going to ask, "Is there anyone you haven't forgiven?" But to get us ready, He asks now. And we need to ask ourselves also, "Does Jesus' kind of love motivate all our attitudes and actions?" If not, what we feel may be Christ's tug on our anchor line. Isn't that gracious of Him? Perhaps that gives us something we need to confess.

⚓ ## The Great Commission

In addition, I believe the judgment of Jesus Christ includes our response to His great commission. He said,

"Go therefore and make disciples of all the nations, baptizing them in the name of the Father and the Son and the Holy Spirit." At that decisive moment of examination in the future, Jesus may ask, "Who is alive forever because of you?"

"Oh, Lord, you don't understand," we might say. "All through my life I didn't want to look religious. I didn't want anyone to put me off because I used religious language. I had to keep my job. I had to stay in my club. I didn't want the neighbors to think I was one of those religious nuts."

But then in my imagination I can hear Jesus ask again, "Who's become a Christian because of you?" And with that question there comes another tug on the anchor line.

The Needs of Others ⚓

Or take Jesus' clear statement about our concern for the physical and social needs of people. Are we distinguished because of that quality?

Lord Anthony Shaftesbury was. After his death, when his funeral cortege moved up Parliament Street to Westminster Abbey, it was followed by hundreds of representatives of the missions, schools, asylums, and charities he had started. They carried banners on which were written Jesus' words about people's needs, "For I was hungry and you gave Me food; I was thirsty and you gave Me drink; I was a stranger and you took Me in. . . . Inasmuch as you did it to one of the least of these My brethren, you did it to Me" (Matt. 25:35, 40). Also a part of that great procession were the poor and disadvantaged Shaftesbury had spent his life helping.

147

Years after Lord Shaftesbury's death, Gladstone was asked to draft an inscription for the humanitarian's monument. He wrote, "He devoted the influence of his station, the strong sympathies of his heart, and the great powers of his mind to honoring God by serving his fellow man."

But Shaftesbury would have written it differently. During his lifetime, he often was heard to say, "My faith may be summed up in one word, and that word is Jesus." There is no doubt that Lord Shaftesbury, long before his death, had passed the Lord's examination about caring for the needs of others. In this he is a model for each of us. Our Christian pilgrimage is to be marked by our concern for the needs of other people, if we are to show that we love as He loved.

At this point, a little further self-examination may be in order as the Lord tugs at our anchor line. What are we doing about the crippling ills in our society—poverty, hunger, AIDS, the homeless? What difference are we making in our world? Here, too, honest confession may be needed.

George Whitefield, the great eighteenth-century preacher, said, "Take care of your life now and the Lord will take care of you when you die." But really, He helps us take care now so that we don't have to worry about where we will spend eternity. That's the assurance of confident hope. Life in Christ is endless hope; without Him life is a hopeless end.

It's a wonderful act of love that Christ holds us accountable and will not let us go. We belong to Him, and He wants us to live every day doing what's really important to Him. That's why He keeps tugging on the anchor line. He wants our attention. Now.

In his novel *Mary Marston*, George McDonald wrote, "I came from God, and I'm going back to God, and I won't have any gaps of death in the middle of my life."

We Can Be Sure

On another sailing occasion after the houseboat experience I related at the beginning of this chapter, an old salt asked me some important questions just before I left the harbor. "There may be a blow. Do you have a storm anchor with a strong line on board? And do you know a good anchorage? You may need both." I assured him I had both my storm tackle and that I knew about a safe anchorage. But when it comes to the ship of my life, I'm even more certain of the sure and steadfast anchor of Christ!

NOTES

1. E. S. Maloney, *Piloting, Steamship and Small Boat Handling,* American Book (New York: Stratford Press, 1977), 89.

Chapter Eight

THE MUSIC AND THE WORDS

Libby Twain, the wife of novelist and humorist Mark Twain, was a proper lady who was always horrified at the amount of profanity her husband wove into his lectures and speeches. One day she decided she was going to cure him.

While tying his string bow tie one night before he left for a lecture, she looked him squarely in the eye, and with a sweet smile on her face she began to swear, using every word she had ever heard her husband use. Finally, she ran out of words, then stopped and waited for his response.

Mark Twain looked down into her eyes, and with a broad smile he said, "Libby, you got the words, but you ain't got the music."

⚓ The Music of Hope

Hope is the music of life. It gives us zest, gusto, and verve. Hope puts a song in our hearts. It not only gets our feet tapping but it gives us the freedom to move out into the "dance of life" with energy and excitement.

Hope is more than words, though. Yes, it is far more than carefully turned phrases or slogans or self-help pep talks. To be real, hope must live inside us. We don't possess hope; hope possesses us. Authentic hope captures us and, at the same time, sets us free.

⚓ Prisoners of Hope

In one of the more obscure books in the Old Testament, God calls His people by a name that describes this captivating, liberating quality of hope. "Return to the stronghold, *you prisoners of hope*" (Zech. 9:12). This magnificent word-portrait is set against the backdrop of the prediction of the coming of two kings, one a human warrior king who would bring destruction, and the other the divine messianic King who would bring salvation.

One hundred years before it happened, God spoke through the prophet Zechariah and predicted the invasion of Alexander the Great and the destruction of Tyre, Sidon, and Gaza. But by God's intervention, Alexander by-passed Jerusalem. Why? Because another King was coming to Jerusalem. The Messiah, King Jesus!

Then, in anticipation of the coming of the Messiah-King, God's people are encouraged to sing and shout,

"Rejoice greatly, O daughter of Zion!
Shout, O daughter of Jerusalem!
Behold, your King is coming to you;
He is just and having salvation,
Lowly and riding on a donkey,
A colt, the foal of a donkey" (Zech. 9:9).

Zechariah's message was addressed to his country-men who were now back in Jerusalem after their years of exile in Babylon. They had indeed been prisoners during those years, but prisoners with a hope, as they had dreamed of Jerusalem. Now these "prisoners of hope" were involved in the rebuilding of their Temple and the Holy City. The prophet Zechariah, whose name means "the Lord remembers," was pointing their way toward their future of hope.

At first, the words "prisoner" and "hope" seem con-tradictory. And yet they belong together when God sets them to the music of His Son. In a way, hope does make us a prisoner. It is true that Christ came to set us free, but in His freedom we are firmly bonded to Him forever. His bond of hope, though, makes us ra-diant, vibrant, singing people. We become tireless, persistent in claiming the Lord's promises in each new day.

It was this idea that prompted George Mattheson, a blind Scots poet and preacher whose life was a song of hope many years ago, to write, "Make me a captive, Lord, and then I shall be free. . . . Imprison me with-in Thine arms, and strong will be my hand."

"Oh, sing to the Lord a new song!" wrote the psalmist, "For He has done marvelous things . . ." (Ps. 98:1). Here is meant not a different song each day, but **155** the same song of hope for each new situation in which we can confidently expect God's presence and power—and freedom!

⚓ Prisoner of the Lord

The most free man who ever lived called himself a "prisoner of the Lord" (Eph. 3:1). Because the Lord had imprisoned Paul with the splendor of hope, he could sing in man-made prisons. His hopeful song and the Lord's intervention at a midnight hour so astounded the Philippian jail keeper that he cried out, "What must I do to be saved?" In response to Paul's answer he and his whole family became Christians.

There were only a few thousand Christians when Paul was converted on the road to Damascus. By the end of his life, the far reaches of the then-known world had heard the gospel from Paul or from those whose lives he had touched with the transforming power of his hope in Christ.

Hope dominated the apostle with single-mindedness in both his prayers and messages. He wrote the Christians at Rome about his prayers for them, "Now may the God of hope fill you with all joy and peace in believing, that you may abound in hope by the power of the Holy Spirit" (Rom. 15:13). He told them that when he came to them, he would share the secret of that abounding, overflowing hope. "But I know that when I come to you, I shall come in the fullness of the blessing of the gospel of Christ" (Rom. 15:29). And what Paul wanted for his Christian friends in Rome is meant for us as well. We are to be people full of hope—and of "music."

156

Go Power

Hope is the go power of the Christian life. It makes everything else work. Somerset Maugham in *Of Human Bondage* says, "Money is like a sixth sense without which you cannot make a complete use of the other five." Of course, that's wide of the mark. But what is on target is that hope is a sixth spiritual sense that fires the five cardinal qualities of the Christian life—faith, love, commitment, vision, and service.

As prisoners of hope—people confident of Christ's indwelling presence and intervention in their needs— we can be irrepressible in our enthusiasm. Our heritage is to live with tiptoe anticipation of what Christ will do for us in the most mundane duties and the most momentous problems of any day. Hope has set us free from berating ourselves over the past or brooding about the future. *We are liberated to live.*

No Hope, No Freedom

Nikos Kazantzakis, the Greek novelist about whom I commented earlier, had his own words placed as an epitaph on his gravestone, "I hope for nothing. I fear nothing. I am free." What a sad way to die and what a horrible way to live. It's the quality of our hope that determines whether we can be fearless and free. The kind of hope Christ releases in our souls frees us from fear of anything or anyone. We are free from the tyranny of "things"—free to follow His will. This freedom keeps our life focus on our primary goal of living every day to love and glorify Him. And we are then free to pursue our secondary goals related to our families or our work.

⚓ ## Measure of Maturity

Karl Menninger, the eminent psychiatrist and Christian, once said, "The hopes we develop are the measure of our maturity." My friend Cliff expresses it this way, "I'd been a baby Christian for years. My idea of hope was simply planning out things, setting my goals and then 'hoping' the Lord would help. I've had some real disappointments and I wondered what was wrong with my prayers or whether or not the Lord was really involved in my life. I got so low that one day I told the Lord I couldn't go on expecting His blessings and receiving so little evidence that He was even around.

"Then one day," Cliff said, "a friend in my Bible study group suggested that I pray for the Lord to guide me in what to ask Him for in whatever I considered my biggest problem. There was no doubt in my mind what that problem was.

"I'd had a strained relationship with my daughter for a long time. She just wasn't living up to my standards. Most of all, she wasn't buying into my kind of Christianity. So I asked the Lord to help me understand what He wanted rather than telling Him what I wanted.

"Over the span of a week, the answer came. It dawned on me that I was the problem! I was holding off loving my daughter until she started doing what I wanted. She was resisting me and not the Lord! When I let go and simply put her in the Lord's hands, boy did my attitude change!

158   "One day over breakfast before she went off to work,

I was struck with the realization of what a lovely daughter I have and that I'd better start enjoying her. A strange new confidence began to grow in me that everything was going to be fine if I just stopped pushing. A new relationship has started to blossom and I've discovered my daughter's a lot closer to Christ than I'd ever realized!"

I was impressed with the progression in Cliff's growth in hope. Before he became a Christian, he was full of wants and needs. When he became a Christian, he started asking the Lord for His help to accomplish his agenda. He called it hope, but he was really just trying to make the Lord his errand boy. Now he's graduated to genuine hope. He's not telling the Lord, but asking what to ask in his prayers. The music of hope, not just the words, has begun in Cliff.

I found the same need for growth in hope in a pastor and a church officer in a church where I spoke recently. During my visit with them, they both told me about their "hope" for their church and about their conflict with each other over what they thought was best. Both of them had a laudable vision, but both needed to love the church and each other more than their vision. They were telling the Lord what to do and doing their best to push their plan. And both had to let go of the self-will that had gotten mixed up with their wishing for the church. When they did, a vision was born that was so much better than either had been holding out for so tenaciously.

In talking with these two men, I shared a quote from Dietrich Bonhoeffer's *Life Together* that seemed to start the music of real hope and freedom in those two men. "Every human wish dream that is injected into the

159

Christian community is a hindrance to genuine community and must be banished if genuine community is to survive. He who loves his dream of a community more than the Christian community itself becomes a destroyer of the latter, even though his personal intentions may be ever so honest and earnest and sacrificial."

Bonhoeffer's insight applies equally to marriage, to friendships, and to all our carefully worked out plans. Not even the programs we develop at work, in the church, or in the community are to become our ultimate hopes. But as we back off and commit our desires to the Lord, He not only refines them but transforms our wishing into real hope. A sure test of hope in Christ is that it enables us to live with deep inner peace and outward freedom.

⚓ Hope on the Creative Edge

Hope is the special gift of the Lord for the creative edge of our lives in which we realize that if anything of lasting value is to be done, *He must do it*. Our only task is to discover what He's doing, where He's breaking through, and then join and follow Him.

And we can be sure that He will lead us into opportunities to serve. Hope is the special gift given to those committed to be servants. Christ came not to be served but to serve. He told His disciples, "Remember the word that I said to you, 'A servant is not greater than his master'" (John 15:20). Christ emulated servanthood and called us to nothing less. When we ask and answer the question "As a servant of Christ and of people, in His name, what can I do to serve unselfishly?" then we

160 can be assured that supernatural power will be released

in us and around us. The assurance of that power gives us the Lord's hope for his agenda of serving.

The Lord Is Working

The music of hope remains stirring and strong inside us when we know that the Lord is working in our relationships and circumstances. I have a desktop eight-by-six-inch computerized dictionary and thesaurus. When I need a definition or synonym, I turn on the computer, type in the word and press the "enter" button. While the computer is scanning its memory bank, the word "working" flashes on the screen. Then in due course, the information is displayed. Sometimes, when it takes awhile, I get impatient and press the "enter" button again, but all I get on the screen is that same word "working."

Prayer is like that. Before the Lord gives us His perfectly timed answer, He flashes the words "I'm working" on the screen of our minds. And, unlike computers that "crash," losing their program or our input, the Lord never forgets and never lets up in His strategy to bring His ultimate goal out of our problems and perplexities.

In the Rough and Tumble

In the rough and tumble of life we constantly need to respond to God's call to "return to the stronghold, *you prisoners of hope.*" For us, it's the stronghold of prayer. And even the desire to pray is His gift. The prophet Isaiah worded it this way, "It shall come to pass that before they call, I will answer; and while they are

161

still speaking, I will hear" (Isa. 65:24). It's in the stronghold that the music of hope grows strong.

The noted preacher and writer Leslie Weatherhead translated Psalm 59:10 in these words:

> My merciful God shall come to meet me
> In a warm and reassuring way:
> My God in His loving kindness,
> Shall meet me at every corner.

We all face corners in life; none of us knows what's around the bend. But prisoners of hope have learned that along with unexpected surprises of difficulty there will also be occasions to meet our gracious Lord of forgiveness and to make new beginnings of innovation and ingenuity. He will be there at the corner with a way to face the problems that we could never have worked out for ourselves. Turn the corner with hope—He's there waiting for you!

David Livingstone was an indefatigable prisoner of hope throughout his years of pushing back the missionary frontiers of Africa. One night, alone beside a treacherous river he had to cross and fearful of attack on the other side, Livingstone heard the music of hope again in his heart. He recorded what happened in his Last Journals. "I heard the words of Jesus again, 'Lo, I am with you always.' I said to myself, 'It is the word of a gentleman of strictest and most sacred honor, and there's the end of it.'" Livingstone forged the river with courage.

⚓ Spendthrift Prisoners

Prisoners of hope are also spendthrifts when it comes to giving themselves and their resources away to those in need. George Moore, a British merchant and philanthropist of another generation, first heard the music of hope when he claimed Jesus' promise, "Most assuredly, I say to you, he who hears My word and believes in Him who sent Me has everlasting life" (John 5:24). From that time on, the foremost quality of his life was the simplicity of his faith and the vitality of his hope in what Christ could do in the lives of people He has called to help.

Each New Year Moore purchased a new diary and inscribed on the flyleaves these words:

> What I spent, I had;
> What I saved, I lost;
> What I gave, I have.

Moore began each year by sending large donations to the charities he had started. Because of his hope, he enjoyed giving. He often was heard to say, "If the world only knew half the happiness that a man has in doing good, it would do a great deal more."

George Moody is a contemporary George Moore. He's head of the Security National Bank and is volunteer Chairman of the Board of the American Red Cross. He's active in dozens of causes in Los Angeles and around the world. His hope is irresistible. He infuses it in people wherever he is. And he's always ready to tell people about the source of his hopefulness in Christ. George stands six feet four inches tall, but he's tallest on his knees. In his office is an open Bible from which he gains his guidance and direction.

With the vibrant theme of hope surging relentlessly **163**

in us, we can never do enough for people and their needs. We don't need money pitches on Stewardship Sunday or slick brochures to convince us to give our money or ourselves.

Early in our century Anglican clergyman and scholar Dean W. R. Inge wrote, "Christianity promises to make us free; it never promises to make us independent." It's in the bond of Christ's hope that we can soar.

One of the moving examples in the Bible about the freedom that grows out of a commitment of love is found in Exodus 21:1-7. It explains the rules for servants in ancient Israel. A servant could serve a Hebrew master for only seven years. During the sixth year, the servant had to be told that in the seventh year he would be released. But if he had taken a wife and had children during his servanthood, he could not take them with him if he left.

The writer of Exodus then goes on to tell what could happen if the servant chose not to be released. "If the servant plainly says, 'I love my master, my wife, and my children; I will not go out free,' then his master shall bring him to the judges. He shall also bring him to the door, or to the doorpost, and his master shall pierce his ear with an awl; and he shall serve him forever" (Exod. 21:5-6).

Our commitment to Christ is like the choice the servant could make. We are at liberty to leave the challenges of being disciples. But we know there's no lasting hope, joy, or peace anywhere else. So we say, "I love my Master, my hope; I will not go out. In being His servant I am free."

We need no awl mark in our ear to identify that we

belong to Christ. A prisoner of hope is unmistakable. Our Master's Spirit is branded on our character. His radiance on our faces is undeniable. Our vision and courage could have no other explanation. And when people listen, they hear the words . . . and the music . . . of hope!

Chapter Nine

HOPEFULLY YOURS

Ken always ends his letters in the same way. "Hopefully yours!" he writes, and then signs his name.

Now, Ken is not simply expressing a wish that the people to whom he is writing will be his friend or perhaps he can be their friend. Rather, he is full of hope for people. So much so, in fact, that those of us who are his close friends have nicknamed him "Hopeful Ken."

For years Ken has kept a "hope list" in the breast pocket of his suit coat. He's never without it and whenever he has a moment's break in his busy life, he pulls it out and goes over it prayerfully. The list doesn't contain his personal needs and wants, however. Instead, it is a list of people who need hope—people in trouble, friends who are bogged down with problems, fellow executives who are running out of steam on the fast track. They're all God's people, but Ken realizes they don't know it. Consequently they are without hope.

Ken prays that he will be given the opportunity of telling the people on his list about Hope Himself, Jesus Christ. As a caring person, Ken always takes the time to listen to the concerns of his friends. He is an authentic communicator of hope.

⚓ Before and After

That didn't used to be the case. When I think back on what Ken was like ten years ago, I'm amazed. He was one of the most negative, cranky, uptight, judgmental, legalistic religious people I'd ever met. He was a leader in his church and his community but had few friends. He was a tyrant at home, a prude at work, and a pharisee in his church.

One day back then Ken came to see me. His tight, little world was falling apart. His wife was threatening to leave him, his children were giving him the stiff arm, his fellow church deacons had turned him off, and things were going badly at work. "Everybody's ganged up on me all at once," Ken said. "I don't know what's happening to me, but everyone is telling me that they are tired of the way I act."

Over several visits, Ken and I got to the core of his need. Though he was a Christian and firmly held to all his orthodox beliefs, he had a very superficial relationship with Christ Himself. As a result, he had no hope for what the Lord could do to change people and transform problems. All he had to go on was his own evaluation of life, his own calculation of what was possible, and his own judgments of people's potential.

"My friend," I said to Ken one day, "You urgently need the gift of hope!" I purposely didn't tell him that

170

he needed a personal experience of Christ's love and forgiveness. He would have turned me off. Leading religious people to a transforming experience of Christ is not easy. So, I talked about the exciting adventure of experiencing hope and becoming a communicator of hope to others.

Ken took the bait. "How do you become that kind of person?" he asked. "That's apparently just the opposite of what I have become."

I shared with Ken the secret of lasting hope we've been talking about in this book. He was especially intrigued by several stories of Christians who, years after becoming believers, had been transformed by Christ's indwelling Spirit. He was taken with the idea that Christ's Spirit is the source of hope. Finally he was ready to admit his own emptiness and need for Christ to indwell his mind and heart.

I'll never forget Ken's prayer of confession as he told the Lord that he wanted to be a caring and sensitive person and a worthy communicator of Christ, the Spirit of hope. He made a commitment to be the most hopeful person he could be by Christ's power.

Ken is now one of those amazing before-and-after examples of what can happen to religious people who allow Christ to love them profoundly and begin to exude hope powerfully. Becoming a communicator of hope saved Ken's marriage. For the first time in fifteen years of life together, his wife felt valued, cherished and affirmed. Eventually, Ken's children believed it was really true that they had a new dad. And with his Christ-filled attitudes his influence is felt widely throughout the community in which he lives and works.

171

⚓ **No Limit**

Believe me, there are no limits to what can happen in our lives when we make a commitment to be communicators of hope and are empowered for that ministry by Hope Himself.

What a boost hopeful people are in our families, places of work, and the church! They take the drabness out of life. My friend Ron Glosser of Akron, Ohio, is an inspirer of hope. When I see him or talk to him on the phone and ask how he is, he responds, "Never better!" He means it, and it's true. Christ is his hope. And that hope is communicated to his employees, at his bank, and in his many social involvements. Hope is not only the motivation for his caring for people's spiritual needs but also for his concern over whatever is bogging them down in their daily lives. I feel refreshed and invigorated every time I talk with Ron.

The secret of Ron's effectiveness is that he keeps close to the Master. His positive attitude is a direct result of that. Ron's model is one we would do well to follow as we picture ourselves as hopeful people in our family setting, among our friends, at work, in church and in the community.

We need to imagine ourselves as vibrantly hopeful persons, thoroughly committed to the Lord, knowing that He can and will transform people and situations. As we prayerfully do this, we will become channels of Christ's hope-oriented, problem-solving power.

⚓ **Our Deepest Need**

Every day I receive hundreds of letters from people telling me about their personal needs. However, I've received very few letters telling me of people's urgent needs to care about what concerns others in their lives and community. That's understandable. We're all concerned about what we believe to be our own needs. But this self-focused concern can keep us from being sensitive to the hurting people around us who are discouraged and without hope.

Christ has called all of us into a ministry of hope. Most of His promises deal with what He will do to empower us in caring for others. And as this happens, we discover that our own growth in hope is inseparably related to the hope we inspire in others. This idea is expressed beautifully by Amy Carmichael.

> Hope through me, God of Hope,
> Or never can I know
> Deep wells and living streams of hope,
> And pools of overflow.
> O blessed Hope of God,
> Flow through me patiently,
> Until I hope for everyone
> As you have hoped for me.[1]

The Greatest Promise

Now, Christ doesn't commission us to be communicators of hope and then leave us out in left field to fend for ourselves. His offer of help comes in this promise: "Whatever you ask in My name, that I will do, that the Father may be glorified in the Son" (John 14:13). To be sure we have grasped the amazing offer He has made, He repeats it even more pointedly, "If you ask anything in My name, I will do it" (v. 14).

That's quite an offer. And yet, this is one of the most misunderstood and misused promises of Christ. It has been the cause of deep disappointment to those who have claimed it without understanding what is involved. Many use this promise only for their own needs. They say, "Whatever I ask, Lord? Anything? Well, let me tell You about my list of desires and problems!" Certainly, the Lord hears and answers our prayers for our own needs, but I wonder if He isn't saddened by the fact that we haven't listened to Him to hear what He said before and after this bold promise to do anything we ask.

⚓ A Promise for the Road

This promise of the Lord's is for the road, for moving on to a ministry of hope for people. Listen to what He promises in the preceding verse. "Most assuredly, I say to you, he who believes in Me, the works that I do he will do also, and greater works than these he will do, because I go to My Father" (John 14:12).

To believe in Christ is to be in caring service for others. There's really no choice about that. We all are called to the bracing challenge of modeling our lives after Jesus' example. That means that we are to love as He loved, forgive as He forgave, heal the physical, emotional and social needs of people as He healed, and to bring hope to the hopeless as He brought hope.

While we are still reeling from that seemingly impossible charge, Christ goes on to tell us that we are also called to do greater works than He did. Greater? What can we do that's greater than the Master could do?

Jesus spoke this promise the night before His crucifixion, three days before His resurrection, and fifty days

before His return to baptize His followers with His
Spirit. At that point, He had converted no one. He had
done miracles and given His revolutionary message of
the kingdom of God. But no one had experienced the
ultimate miracle of becoming a new creation or had entered the kingdom. That required the liberation of the
cross, the regeneration of the resurrection, and the em-
powering of Pentecost when the Holy Spirit came to
indwell the lives of His people—people just like you
and me.

So the "greater works" that we are to do are to communicate the hope of our victorious Lord and introduce people to Him. And, with the Lord living in us,
the works that He did as Jesus of Nazareth are to be
done by His power as everyday Christianity.

Staggering? Yes! "But how, Lord?" we ask. His response is, "I've been waiting for you to ask. Now you
can appreciate My promise 'If you ask anything in My
name, I will do it.'"

Prayer Is the Link ⚓

Prayer is the link between the hope Christ offers us
and the hopelessness of people around us. Actually, we
are to spend more time talking to the Lord about people than we spend talking to people about the Lord!
When we do, two things happen.

First, we are given the Lord's eyes to see people as He
sees them and His heart to love them as He loves them.
Because each person is unique, He gives us His special
strategy for communicating His hope for each one.

Second, when we pray for someone, the Lord intensifies His preparation of that person to receive His   175

hope. He will arrange circumstances to confront people with their need for Him. He will work in their minds and hearts creating a new openness.

But we need to remember that the Lord's timing is not always ours. So we must leave the "when" to Him —and also the "how." He may use us or someone else. That's really not important. Our task is to be ready and available while we persist in prayer.

⚓ Freedom from Stress and Strain

Many of our stresses have to do with people who do not have hope. They are in our families, among our friends, at our places of work, in our churches—everywhere! They produce pressure, worry, conflict and frustration for themselves and for others. Most likely they act the way they do because of their flat, horizontal view of their own potential and of life's possibilities.

Specifically asking the Lord to enable such persons for whom we are concerned to experience His hope-Spirit removes the stress and strain from us. People without hope have little or no expectation of what Christ is capable of doing to help them or to invade their grim circumstances. Some of them become even more determined to manipulate the world around them. The danger is that we may fall into the trap of overreacting to what they do rather than redoubling our prayer for their real need to experience lasting hope.

⚓ A Call to Love

A quick review of Christ's commandments reminds us that they are essentially a call to love. "A new

176

commandment I give to you, that you love one another; as I have loved you, that you also love one another. By this all will know that you are My disciples, if you have love for one another" (John 13:34–35). This commandment was given earlier in Jesus' conversation with the disciples in the Upper Room.

Later that same night, He repeated the commandment to love with a special emphasis on the fruit our love for others is to bear. "You did not choose Me," He said, "but I chose you and appointed you that you should go and bear fruit, and that your fruit should remain, that whatever you ask the Father in My name He may give you. These things I command you, that you love one another" (John 15:16–17).

We are to bear fruit, and the fruit of the Christian is the lives of people we influence and introduce to authentic hope. We are to be reproductive, and the way we are to do that is to love. So when we commit ourselves to do Christ's works, we can claim the promise that Christ will answer our prayers for them.

Hope for the People Who Need Hope

The Lord answers our prayer by giving us hope for the very people we are called to love. That's crucial, because without hope our faith is stunted and our love is stymied. Christ's hope in us implements courageous faith and instigates caring love.

Without His hope it is impossible to have faith in what Christ can do for the people for whom we are praying. Hope activates our basic faith in Christ into a daring faith. Faith forms the picture of what we can expect and hope believes that in the Lord's timing it shall be true. Hope gives us what the great Danish Christian Sören Kierkegaard called the "passion for what is possible." It expands the horizons of what we claim by faith.

⚓ The Inseparable Companion

John Calvin, the impassioned Christian reformer, emphasized the crucial role of hope for kindling our faith. In his *Institutes of the Christian Religion,* he said that hope is the inseparable companion of faith.

> When this hope is taken away, however eloquently or elegantly we discourse concerning faith, we are convicted of having none. Hope is nothing else than the expectation of those things which faith has believed to have been truly promised by God . . . . Hope nourishes and sustains faith . . . . For no one except him who already believes His promises can look for anything from God, so again the weakness of our faith must be sustained and nourished by hope and expectation, lest it fail and grow faint . . . . By unremitting renewing and restoring, it [hope] invigorates faith again and again with perseverance.[2]

German theologian Jürgen Moltmann, in his benchmark work on hope, *The Theology of Hope,* puts it this way:

> Thus, in the Christian life faith has the priority, but hope the primacy. Without faith's knowledge of Christ, hope becomes a utopia and remains hanging in the air. But without hope, faith falls to pieces, becomes fainthearted and ultimately a dead faith. It is through faith that a man finds the path of true life, but it is only hope

that keeps him on that path. Thus it is that faith in Christ gives hope its assurance. Thus it is that hope gives faith in Christ its breadth and leads it into life.[3]

Hope and Love

Hope is also the inseparable companion of love. It is impossible to love people unless we have hope for them. When we lose hope in what Christ can accomplish in them, we become incapable of loving.

Notice that I said "what Christ can accomplish." The ground of our hope for people is not what we can do to change them, but what Christ can do. Our task is to fall in line with what He guides us to say and do and leave the results to Him.

Practical Expressions

We can cooperate with the Lord in some very practical expressions of love. For example, we can begin by letting people know that we are for them. Hope inspires that quality of love in spite of what people have been or are doing. We can affirm people by words and actions that tell them we believe in them.

But that can't be done from a distance. We must become involved in giving ourselves, our time, and our resources to help them. Putting judgments aside, we are called to give esteem and positive reinforcement to other people.

Remember how it happened to us. We could not change what we were until someone loved us as we were and gave us the confidence to dare to be different. And the Lord probably used a hope-filled person to

179

love us to the place where we could ask for help to begin again.

⚓ Hope for a Hopeless Cocaine Addict

Linda is a good example of how this works. A year ago, she was a hopeless cocaine addict. Her addiction had caused serious health problems, including a heart attack. She was in despair, wondering what would happen to her and her young son.

One Sunday morning she wandered into our church and sat in the balcony weeping through the service. She heard the good news of Christ's love and forgiveness and how to make a new start. Most of all, she felt the Savior's love from the people around her in the pews.

Linda returned week after week, but each time she was reluctant to fill out the visitors' registration slip in the bulletin. Finally one Sunday, when she was at rock bottom, she filled out the visitors' slip, saying she needed help, and gave it to an usher.

One evening during the following week, she was called on by one of our Night of Caring calling teams. An elder in our church, Fred Gruberth, was one member of the two-member team. Fred has the gift of hope as well as profound love. He's an active participant in our prayer and healing ministry, and he quickly discerned Linda's urgent need for Christ. He was determined that he and his fellow caller would remain with her until she received the Lord's love and healing. Fred explained how Linda could meet Christ and waited patiently until she committed her life to Christ and asked for His healing of her addiction.

180   I met Linda some months later when she appeared

before our church elders to make a public confession of her faith and join the church. She told the story of what had happened to her, radiating joy as she shared with all of us her victory over addiction to cocaine.

After the meeting, I had a personal visit with Linda. Free of drugs, she's a vibrant, attractive young woman. "I want to share what I've found," she said with enthusiasm. "I want to work with young people who are experimenting with drugs and with people hooked on hard drugs. I want them to know there's hope!" We quickly got her in touch with a member of our church, Priscilla Davis, of the Christian Jail Workers. Now she's helping teenagers who are addicted and need Christ's hope.

Hope for All Kinds of People ⚓

But Linda was not the only person who appeared before our church elders that night to confess Christ. In fact, there was a large class of new members. Singles, couples, businesspeople, actors and actresses, professionals of all kinds, and laborers. All had been part of an eight-week Inquirers' Class led by Scott Erdman, our Pastor of Evangelism. During these eight weeks each person is assigned to what is called a Caring Cluster, a small group for discussion and for sharing in the experience of mutual love and encouragement. Also, everyone was given a Guardian Angel, a member of the church who was to help in the class member's spiritual growth.

I was thrilled as I listened to the testimonies of those new members. All of them had made a fresh start in the faith and so many said that in their Caring Cluster or 181 with their Guardian Angel they had found new hope. As I drove home that evening after this exciting meeting, I prayed, "Thank You, Lord, That's what a church of hope is meant to be!"

The next day, I reflected on all the people I know who need the hope these new and renewed believers had received. Some of them are Christians, but have little hope. Then I thought about their friends and loved ones around them who have not been able to communicate the hope in Christ they need.

That made me wonder: Which is worse—to not have experienced hope yet, or to have hope and not communicate it? Both are sad and neither is what Christ desires. Instead He wants a renewal movement in which every Christian is a communicator of hope. And that will start when you and I say, "Lord, start with me. Renew Your hope in me and then put me in touch with those You've put on my agenda. Show the way. I'm ready!"

Recently, Mary Jane was preparing for a talk at a women's retreat at our church, where she was to speak on the calling of a mother, mother-in-law, and grandmother. As part of her preparation, she asked each of our children and our daughter-in-law and our son-in-law what she had done or was doing right and what she had done or should do differently. It takes courage to ask questions like that. But it was Mary Jane's turn to receive some bouquets of affirmation. The kids overflowed with memories of the way their mom had always been there for them, listening, hurting when they hurt, and applauding their successes. Most of all, she had given them an example of hope. Things were never so tough that she lost hope in what the Lord was doing in them. And in the small and big victories in their

182

lives, she seemed to take even greater delight than they did. They named her their cheerleader.

"Lloyd," Mary Jane said to me later, "it's all been worth it! I really have had a boost talking to the kids. They have given me a gift to last me the rest of my life!" And why not—she's been their booster for years.

Your Hope List

Earlier I wrote about my friend Ken's hope list, on which he had written the names of people for whom he felt he needed to pray. There's a direct relationship between Ken's prayers and his effectiveness as a communicator of hope.

We all need a hope list. Do you have one? I do. It's kept close to my Bible, for daily reference in my prayer time. What a delight it is to keep a log on the amazing ways the Lord answers. Some names have been on my list for a long time. But I can't give up on those people. Christ hasn't, so how can I?

Take time to make up your own hope list of people. Pray for them, claiming Christ's promise to answer. Then be prepared to be part of the answer. Be sure of your own hope and then be willing to share that hope in an open, caring way.

Peter gives us the progression for our ministry of hope. "But sanctify the Lord God in your hearts, and always be ready to give a defense to everyone who asks you a reason for the hope that is in you, with meekness and fear . . . ." (1 Pet. 3:15). This advice was for the early Christians who faced trial and persecution, but it applies to us as well. In a different way our hope is on trial. People are watching to see whether that hope

183

makes any difference in how we live in the ups and downs of life.

And when we're given the opportunity to share our hope, we are to do it with meekness. The word "meek" describes a person who, out of love and obedience, openly accepts Christ's guidance and direction. In classical Greek, the word was used to describe an animal that had been tamed and brought under the control of the bit and reins and had learned to follow the commands of its master. Meek communicators of hope are those who are under Christ's lordship. They are not arrogant or proud, but humble and winsome, because they know that the source of their hope is not in themselves but in Christ. They live with the certainty of Christ's power and presence.

Peter also tells us that we are to communicate our hope with fear. What does that mean for us today? It certainly does not mean that we are to share our hope with panic. What it does mean, as we said earlier, is that we realize that we are accountable to the Lord for what we do with the opportunities He gives us to witness to the power of His hope in us. It is awesome to realize that we could miss those crucial times because we are too busy or insensitive to the opportunity. When someone's eternal life may be at stake, that does send a shudder up our spines. That makes us all the more alert for the next opportunity.

A Six-Way Test

A good way to evaluate our own effectiveness as communicators of hope is to respond to the following six-way test.

1. Would the people in your life see you as a hopeful thinker with a positive attitude?
2. In difficult situations at home, work, church or in the community, would you be one of the first people to whom others would turn for hope? Have they in the past?
3. Can you name ten people for whom you are praying that they will receive the gift of hope?
4. When's the last time you shared your hope with someone?
5. What are the specific relationships or situations ahead this week in which you could be a communicator of hope?
6. What would you do differently if being a hope-inspirer were one of the primary goals of your life?

Well, how did you do? I don't know about you, but those questions have led me to a new commitment to communicate hope. It's very exhilarating to think about what it might be like to be "Hopefully yours!"

NOTES

1. Amy Carmichael, "Edges of His Ways," *Selections for Daily Reading, From the Notes of Amy Carmichael* (Fort Washington, Pa.: Christian Literature Crusade, 1903[4]), 144.
2. John Calvin, "Institute III 2.42 ET," *Institutes of the Christian Religion*, Library of Christian Classics, vols. 20 and 21, comp. John T. McNeill, trans. Ford Lewis Battles (Philadelphia: Westminster Press, 1961), 590.
3. Jürgen Moltmann, *The Theology of Hope* (London: SCM Press, 1967), 20.

Chapter Ten

HOW
TO BE
HAPPY
ALL OF THE TIME

Erin and Airley, my little granddaughters, are happy children. Well, most of the time.

One exception is when they have to endure the long wait while family portraits are being taken. I'll never understand why it takes a photographer so long to adjust the camera speed, get the lights right, and rearrange the girls' dresses before he can take the picture.

Their mother Eileen has learned how to handle this problem. Just before the photographer clicks the picture, she says, "Happy!" and Erin and Airley go into action. They put on clown faces, clap their hands, and exude their customary happiness. The result is that Mary Jane and I have dozens of albums filled with pictures of full-of-fun, giggling, clowning granddaughters.

Wouldn't it be wonderful if simply saying the word "happy" could make you and me really happy? And we all can think of people we know who look unhappy **189** most of the time. Wouldn't it be great if a one-word reminder—"Happy!"—would inspire them to look happy? But we know from our own personal pursuit of happiness how disconcerting it is for someone to say to us, "You are looking very unhappy. Just pretend you are happy, and soon it will be so!" At such moments we wish they could be more sensitive to the things inside us that make us feel unhappy.

That's how June felt when she and her husband, Sam, got into their car to drive off to Palm Springs for a week's vacation. Before Sam turned on the ignition, he said, "Okay, lady, you're unhappy nearly all the time, but I want you to be happy for these next seven days!"

Later June confessed, "I got myself all wound up and did my best to be happy all through that week. But when we got back home, I crashed. I'd like to be able to blame Sam, the kids, our house—but I know something else is wrong. I'm not really a happy person inside. And being told I ought to be happy doesn't help."

Unless I miss my guess, you may have felt a little put off by the title of this chapter, "How to Be Happy All of the Time." You may have thought, "Oh, come on, Lloyd, don't hold out a promise like that. It's really impossible to be happy all of the time. You don't know what I'm facing right now that makes me feel unhappy!"

To that I would have to respond, "Yes, I do." In talking with people every day and in reading the hundreds of letters from television viewers that come to me every week, I am very aware of the perplexing problems and difficult relationships that are causing them unhappiness. Many of them are suffering physical pain. Others are reeling from the shock of losing a loved one and are wondering what to do with their grief and loneliness.

Still others have faced great disappointments with people, their jobs, and unrealized dreams.

But there's another and more personal reason for my response—I'm trying to be honest about my own set of needs. I know how often I'm tempted to think that if I could just once get all the work finished that is staring me in the face, and if all my relationships were in apple-pie order, then I could be happy. But I know life isn't like that. There'd be a long wait for happiness, because it's always just when I think I'm about to get everything nailed down that something else comes loose.

A generalized prognosis from one of my physical therapists during the long period of healing of my crushed leg really shocked me. She said something I suspect that she had said often to lots of patients, "Don't rush things. It will be over a year before you are back to being your old happy self." The comment prompted a deep conversation about having true happiness in trying circumstances rather than waiting for it at the end of that period.

That conversation was still on my mind as I talked long distance with my friend Roger. I've been privileged to be his prayer partner through some very tough times of financial crisis for him. Roger reported that he was now sure he was going to survive. Then he said, "Lloyd, I've put happiness on hold through all this. Now that the crisis is passed, I ought to be happy, but I'm not. As a matter of fact, I've gotten so used to being unhappy through this mess that it's difficult to relax and be happy again. I was really startled the other day when my wife said, 'Roger, now we have a hope for happiness.'"

Of course, we all know what Roger's wife meant by **191**

her encouraging comment, but she had used the word "hope" carelessly. She and Roger weren't about to have hope for happiness just because the crisis was passed; what they needed was an authentic hope that could give them unassailable happiness regardless of what they had to go through in the future.

⚓ Our Hope for Happiness

Real hope and true happiness are inseparable. I'm not talking about a humanly induced kind of happiness. Rather, I'm affirming a constant experience of Christ-inspired hope that can make us truly happy all of the time. Happiness doesn't need to be an on-again, off-again experience. But lasting happiness is putting our roots down into the limitless flow of God's hope-saturated joy.

Jeremiah vividly described how we become rooted in God's joy: "Blessed is the man who trusts in the Lord, and whose hope is the Lord" (Jer. 17:7). Throughout the Bible the word "blessed" is used to capture a special quality of happiness. The Hebrew word for "blessed" actually means "acclamation." In the Old Testament, blessedness is inseparable from belonging to God, knowing we are His beloved, and receiving His spiritual and material blessings. It means being called, chosen, loved, forgiven, cherished, and cared for with His timely provision.

"Blessed" is a description of an intimate relationship between God and a person who trusts in Him and experiences hope. The same Hebrew word is also translated as "happy" in Psalm 144:15: "Happy are the people whose God is the Lord!"

Jeremiah goes on to give us an impelling metaphor for how we are to be blessed, happy. We are to be "like a tree planted by the waters, which spreads out its roots by the river." The vivid picture is of a tree that has been transplanted and re-rooted by a flowing river. The Hebrew word for "spreads out" means that the roots push out relentlessly, intentionally, and persistently until they reach the river bed. The tree then draws from the unlimited resources of the river. As a result it becomes stable, strong, and stately in spite of winds and storms.

In Scripture the river is a magnificent metaphor for the Spirit of the Lord. The term "rivers of water" is used often for His presence and power. The psalmist speaks of the "river whose streams shall make glad the city of God" (Ps. 46:4). Ezekiel writes, "Everything will live wherever the river goes." Jesus promised a "fountain of water springing up into everlasting life" (John 4:14) and then made this bold claim, "If anyone thirsts, let him come to Me and drink. He who believes in Me, as the Scripture has said, out of his heart shall flow rivers of living water" (John 7:37–38).

The river of life for us is the living Christ, God's presence with us. His promise of rivers of living water, coupled with Jeremiah's image of the tree with roots pressed into the river, gives us the secret of ever-flowing happiness. Christ's spirit is like a river from which we draw hope and joy. Then, following Jeremiah's imagery, with our roots in the river, we will be like a tree that does not "fear when heat comes, but her leaf will be green, and will not be anxious in the year of drought, nor will cease from yielding fruit." In other words, our blessedness, our happiness, will not be diminished by changing circumstances, difficulties,   **193** or adversities, but will be as consistent as the hope and joy of the river of Christ's spirit. John Newton worded this idea beautifully in his hymn "Glorious Things of Thee Are Spoken."

Who can faint when such a river
Ever flows their thirst to assuage?
Grace which, like the Lord the Giver,
Never fails from age to age!

⚓ Roots in the River

But an honest confession of many of us would have to be that we are fainting because our roots are not in the river of life. The river is flowing, but we are not drawing its renewing power daily, hour by hour.

Our unhappy times alert us to our need. We have the roots of our souls in circumstances and relationships and try to draw our meaning from them. But we were meant to bring happiness to our surroundings, not find our ultimate happiness in them. Whenever we demand that people, our families, our jobs, our church, our possessions make us happy, eventually we will be disappointed.

People do let us down. Why are we surprised? We know that we have failed others repeatedly. Should we expect more from them than we have been able to produce ourselves? And who hasn't staked his or her life on finding happiness in some activity, position, or accomplishment, only to find that these things didn't produce lasting happiness?

Any time we feel unhappy, we need to trace the
194 mood back to its cause. That means going beyond the

people or situations that may be the focus of our unhappiness. It requires that we probe until we get back to the point at which we stopped drawing water from the river of life. If happiness is joy expressed *in* our circumstances and relationships, and if joy is the result of hope that comes by grace, then our unhappiness can be cured only by fresh infilling of the spirit of Christ.

So when a mood of unhappiness envelopes us, we can do three things. First, we refuse to blame any person or situation. Second, we tell the Lord how we feel. He's an expert in dealing with unhappy people—He's been helping them for thousands of years. Third, in His loving, forgiving presence, we can gratefully praise Him for all He's done for us on Calvary and all through the years. Let's glorify Him for His faithfulness.

When we do that we will feel loved. New hope will spring up in us. Joy will replace the grimness that we've been feeling. And that joy will exude in a fresh attitude of happiness regardless of whether things or people around us change or remain the same. We will be new persons even though we are in old surroundings.

Knowing We Are Blessed

What I've just described is the experience of the "blessing." It's the most precious gift we can receive from having our roots in the "river." True happiness is knowing that we are blessed.

Now, I'm not talking about material things or success. The blessing is so much more than these. It is the affirmation and the confirmation from the Lord that we are chosen, cherished, and valued. Feeling blessed is like knowing you are the "grace child" of your parents, **195** the one child in the family singled out to receive special approbation, encouragement and cheers.

Many people didn't feel blessed by their parents. Often those parents felt unblessed themselves and were unable to bless their children. But because of this, people who feel unblessed will spend a whole lifetime searching for the blessing, looking for someone to love them, attempting to accomplish something to assure themselves they are of value.

But when we put our roots into the river, all that is changed. We begin to feel like the "grace child" of our Heavenly Father. He says, "Behold, I make all things new. . . . It is done! I am the Alpha and the Omega, the Beginning and the End. I will give of the fountain of the water of life freely to him who thirsts. He who overcomes shall inherit all things, and I will be his God and he shall be My son" (Rev. 21:5-7).

That promise is constantly repeated for us each day. Christ, the Water of Life, ensures it. He reaffirms our status as a blessed child of the Father. Daily He reissues His call to us, mediates cherishing love, reminds us of His delight in us. And His Spirit in us helps us to claim the Father's tender care.

Perhaps, as you read this, you are not feeling very much like a "grace child." Your problems and difficulties may have made you feel more like a rejected child of the Father. It happens to all of us at times. We have become so accustomed to thinking of the Father's love in terms of the things we want Him to give us and of a trouble-free life. Prayer becomes a gimme game, "Do you love me, or do you not? If you love me, give me what I want!" A perilous division between the gift and the Giver is created. Soon we want God's provision more than His presence. Our roots turn from the river to the desert. Eventually, our happiness withers.

A Faucet or a Reservoir ⚓

Or, to shift the metaphor slightly, we confuse the faucet of prayer with the reservoir of hope and joy. There's a wonderful story from the life of Lawrence of Arabia that points up this confusion. When Lawrence took some Arabian chieftains to Paris for the Paris Peace Conference, they were astounded by the conveniences of the city. What they found most amazing of all was the running water that flowed from the faucets in their hotel rooms. Life in the desert had taught them the scarcity and the value of water. But now by simply turning on the faucet, they could have all of the water they wanted. They drank it, bathed in it, and still there was more.

When it came time for Lawrence and his party to check out of their hotel rooms, he found the Arab chieftains doing a curious thing. They were trying to detach the faucets so they could take them with them to the desert. He tried to explain that the faucets were useless without being connected to the pipes which were in turn attached to the water mains leading to the city's reservoirs. But the Arabs would not be dissuaded. They really believed that if they had the magic faucets in the desert, they would have an endless supply of water!

We laugh at the absurdity of the assumption that faucets are the source of the water they produce. But my laughter catches like a bone in my throat when I reflect on the implications of this parable. So often we think of prayer as the magic faucet assuring us that we will get a continuous supply of what we want when we want it from God. Sometimes we pray when by our actions and attitudes we've already closed the water main. The water in the pipes is soon drained off. For a time we endure little more than a drip from it and then exist with nothing more than the rattle of air in the empty pipes. It would be absurd to blame the faucet when the problem is that the main leading to the reservoir is closed!

We turn the water main back on when we accept again the full blessing of being loved, accepted and forgiven. Then we can draw a fresh supply of the Spirit to strengthen us in each moment of need. The reservoir of hope is full to overflowing. Our happiness is dependent on keeping the main line to the faucet of prayer opened.

⚓ New Happiness Every Morning

I've discovered that a happy life is made up of a succession of happy days. Each must begin with a fresh supply of the hope-saturated joy we've been talking about. Jeremiah, who gave us the metaphor of the river, also confided how he drew on its resources at the beginning of every day. In Lamentations 3:21–24, he tells us, "This I recall to mind, therefore I have hope. Through the Lord's mercies we are not consumed, because His compassions fail not. They are new every morning; great is Your faithfulness. 'The Lord is my portion,' says my soul, 'therefore, I hope in Him!'"

A sure way to reverse the drift into feeling unhappy about life is to begin each day with a quiet time of praise
198   to the Lord for His mercy, compassion, and faithfulness.

That renews our assurance that we are blessed people. We are filled with a happy attitude toward the day ahead, knowing that nothing, of itself, can rob us of the joy of the Lord.

'Tis Dear ⚓

On the way to the northwest coast of Scotland where I had my accident, I stopped at a jewelry store in Fort William to look for a piece of Ogilvie clan memorabilia to bring home to Mary Jane. What I found was very expensive.

"Aye, 'tis dear, but then, 'tis for a dear one," the clerk said, making a play on the word "dear" for my American ears. In Scotland the word is used to mean either expensive or cherished.

The clerk was right on both counts. The rare piece of memorabilia was very dear and buying it would require forgoing other things. And it most certainly would be for a dear one—my love, best friend and teammate, my wife, Mary Jane.

"So, you think my wife is expensive . . ." I said, with a smile, throwing back the man's double entendre to him.

Not to be outdone, he replied with a twinkle in his eye, "Only you'd know what she's worth, sir."

He had me! I made the purchase with happy abandonment. Little did I know that in several days I would be lying in a hospital bed there with a crushed leg.

The words, "'Tis dear, but then, 'tis for a dear one," kept coming back to me during my long period of recovery back home. Strange, isn't it, how the words of a song or someone's casual remark will keep tumbling around in our minds?

I had lots of reasons during my convalescence to reaffirm how dear Mary Jane is to me. Those months gave us time for long talks. And humanly speaking, I could not have made it without her love and constant encouragement.

But the words of the clerk took on even greater meaning as I thought about the most dear One in my life—Hope Himself, Christ, my Lord. During those long, painful and difficult days of recovery, I had lots of time to think about how gracious He had been to me.

The Lord had saved my life, as I have described. He had found me in a lonely, desolate place and had given me strength and courage to drag myself to the road where three angels of mercy could discover me just in time. There were really four: to use Nebuchadnezzar's words, there was also "a fourth, one like the Son of God."

When I reflected on that, it occurred to me how often the Lord has refound me since we first met when I was a freshman in college—times when I'd tried to handle things on my own, faced what seemed like impossible challenges, or became overly involved in secondary things. Quite honestly, I had to reword the refrain from the hymn "Amazing Grace" to, "I've often gotten lost and always have been refound."

And so, as I put my roots down deeper in the rivers of living water during my convalescence, I could say, "Dear Lord" with a great deal more depth of gratitude. In a way that was neither overly sentimental nor subjective, Christ became more dear to me than ever—loved,

200

cherished, highly honored, valued. And in a renewed way, I knew I was dear to Him.

A Fresh Draft of Living Water ⚓

The hope-saturated joy we've been talking about in this chapter flowed from the river as I thought about two of my favorite parables, the hidden treasure and the pearl of great price. I'd spoken and written about them often in the past. But now they provided a fresh draft of the water of life.

I got inside the sweaty skin of that plowman faithfully plowing the field. He had been at work all day under the blazing sun. When his plow hit what he thought was another big rock, he set it aside, stooped down, and began digging with his hands to uncover and remove the obstruction. When he finally had it uncovered, he discovered that it was not a rock at all but a treasure chest! He knew that sometimes people had buried their gold, silver and precious jewels in chests like that and left them in the ground until they could return and claim it again.

The plowman looked around. Did anyone see him make his great discovery? No. He quickly closed the treasure chest, covered it with dirt and carefully marked the spot. Then an idea formed in his mind. "I must have this field and possess this treasure. Everything I have is worth it!," he said to himself with uncontainable excitement.

Next the plowman went out and sold everything he had and bought the field. The priceless treasure was his!

While Jesus' disciples were still grappling with the meaning of this attention-riveting parable, He went on **201** with a similar one about a merchant in search of beautiful pearls—one pearl, in particular, probably. Perhaps it was one of the lost twin pearls of Cleopatra, valued at four hundred thousand dollars then. The merchant had heard that this pearl was now being bartered in the bazaars of the world. Tales of its matchless beauty intensified the longing of every merchant to get a look at it. But to handle it . . . and to own it?

No wonder the disciples were quickly caught up in Jesus' parable. It took only thirty-one words for Jesus to tell, but they never forgot it. They could imagine the stunned merchant when he saw the pearl of pearls. He had searched for that pearl all his life. No price would be too high, no sacrifice too much. He liquidated all his assets to buy the pearl. He had found and purchased the pearl of limitless value. And now it belonged to him!

What was Jesus driving at in those two parables? What was He really trying to communicate to the disciples—and, now, to us?

⚓ Two Interpretations

The first of two possible interpretations is the most obvious and most widely held. It is that the kingdom of God—His rule and reign in us, between us, and in all of life—is of surpassing value. Like the plowman's found treasure and the merchant's discovered pearl, it is worth giving all we have and are to enter it.

But doesn't something have to happen before we can do that? I think so. What that happening is comes through a second interpretation.

202   This calls for us to look back at what happened just

before Jesus told these stories. The disciples had asked the Master to explain another parable, the one about the wheat and the tares that He had told when teaching the crowd. When the disciples had Him alone, they wanted to know what He had meant by the account of the sower who had sown good seeds in a field, only to have an enemy come afterward and sow tares, or weeds. It was only after the seeds had sprouted and grown that the weeds could be identified, rooted out, and burned.

The important thing is that, in His response to the disciples' questions, Jesus clearly identified Himself as the Sower of the good seed and the field as the world. Then immediately He told the parable of the treasure. The metaphor of the field would not change. The field being plowed was the world. And the plowman? Like the sower, Jesus Himself. Then, without losing a breath, He gave the parable of the pearl. Who is the merchant? Again, it is Jesus.

Dynamic Hope

Now we are on the edge of the source of dynamic hope. The most important question is, what is the treasure, the pearl? Not what, but who? It was the disciples, it is you and I! And the treasure? Many years before, God had said that His people are "a special treasure to Me among all people" (Exod. 19:5). The psalmist sang the same theme: "For the Lord has chosen Jacob for Himself, Israel for His special treasure" (Ps. 135:4).

Jesus Christ, the eternal hope in the heart of God, came in search of lost humanity, and men and women were the pearl of inestimable value to Him—all part of the lost treasure of a creation separated from the   203

Father, whom Jesus compared with the father in the parable of the prodigal son. The timeless parables and stories of the Master, along with the rolling thunder of His Sinai-like declarations as the very Word of God, made one truth undeniably clear—He had come to save lost humankind.

Christ had been one with the Father when we were made in their image. He knew what we were meant to be and what we had done with the glorious destiny of being daughters and sons of God. And Hope Himself came with unquenchable confidence that we were worth buying back.

The scientist Hendrik Van Loon once remarked, "Ours is a fifth rate planet revolving around a tenth rate sun in a forgotten corner of the universe." Christ's incarnate life denies that depreciating putdown. There may be other universes, but God is sovereign of all of them. And the world and all of us in it are no forgotten corner of this universe, even though many on earth try to forget that He's in charge.

⚓ Remembering the Lord Never Forgets

We all need reminding of this eternal truth. I did often during my year of recovery. When I was in bed wondering when I could walk again, my friend Joy Eilers sent me a photograph she had found among her mother's things after she died. It was a picture she had taken of the large, lighted sign on the corner of our church where my sermon titles and name are displayed. She had taken the picture years before on a Sunday I'd preached on the topic "The Lord Never Forgets." The custodian who had arranged the letters on the sign that week had put my name immediately below. There were no quotation marks, so it all read as one: *The Lord Never Forgets Lloyd Ogilvie.* And when I really needed to be reminded of that, a cheery note with the photograph arrived.

But it's what Christ our hope did for us that makes us sure that He never forgets. He went to the cross to redeem us. The word is drenched with hope throughout the New Testament. The same word for "bought" in the parables of the treasure and the pearl is the word that's used often in the Epistles and the Book of Revelation to describe Christ's death for us.

The apostle Paul emphasized this truth when he wrote, "For you were bought at a price; therefore glorify God in your body" (1 Cor. 6:20). And Peter talks about those who refused to claim their redemption, denying "the Lord who bought them" (2 Pet. 2:1). John, too, joins with the chorus of heaven in praise for Christ's finished mission. "You are worthy . . . for You . . . have redeemed us to God by Your blood out of every tribe and tongue and people and nation, and have made us kings and priests to our God . . ." (Rev. 5:9–10a). The same word John uses for "redeemed" is the one used for "bought" in the other verses.

Hopeful Treasure

We are the treasure and the pearl. We are treasured and the cost of the cross is the price paid by our Lord to make us His own again. In a sense, He sold all that He had, gave it up temporarily, so we could experience His love and forgiveness. Hope begins at Calvary, or it

205

has no beginning; it's given wings beside an empty tomb, or it never soars; it's given power in a personal repetition of Pentecost, or it has no staying strength; and it is the endowment of the indwelling Christ, or it has no endurance. We treasure Christ and His kingdom because we have been treasured.

I'm no poet, but here are some lines that bring it together for me:

Knowing you are the Lord's treasure,
Vibrant hope will grow without measure.
When you make the Lord your treasure,
Lasting hope will replace all conjecture.

To know that we've been found by Christ does release us from guessing about either our value or our purpose. And being refound in the midst of any of the tragedies, illnesses, or mishaps of life intensifies our commitment to be more intentional disciples simply because we know we've been loved and given a second—or a hundredth—chance.

Then we can accept how "dear" it is to be Christ's disciples. It is costly. Being His unreserved, loyal, faithful followers comes at the high price of committing ourselves completely to take up our cross and follow Him. Yet, it's not religious drudgery, but a delight.

Everything from praying and witnessing to living out our faith in social problems is done with the motivation of love. And so is everything from paying the bills to settling a squabble with the kids, from carrying out the garbage to staying up all night with a troubled friend, and from making tough decisions to loving the people

who frustrate us or coping with the difficulties that try

our patience. In it all, there's an indomitable kind of happiness.

"'Tis dear, but then, 'tis for a dear One."

The other day a friend asked, "Now that you've been healed and given the second half of your life to live, what are you going to do with it?"

There was no hesitation in my response, "Accept the gift of Hope Himself, draw on His limitless resources every moment, and run with Him on two strong legs."

The Lord has plans for you and me. We have hope . . . and a future!

CHRISTIAN HERALD
People Making a Difference

Christian Herald is a family of dedicated, Christ-centered ministries that reaches out to deprived children in need, and to homeless men who are lost in alcoholism and drug addiction. Christian Herald also offers the finest in family and evangelical literature through its book club and publishes a popular, dynamic magazine for today's Christians.

Our Ministries

Christian Herald Children. The door of God's grace opens wide to give impoverished youngsters a breath of fresh air, away from the evils of the streets. Every summer, hundreds of youngsters are welcomed at the Christian Herald Mont Lawn Camp located in the Poconos at Bushkill, Pennsylvania. Year-round assistance is also provided, including teen programs, tutoring in reading and writing, family counseling, career guidance and college scholarship programs.

The Bowery Mission. Located in New York City, the Bowery Mission offers hope and Gospel strength to the downtrodden and homeless. Here, the men of Skid Row are fed, clothed, ministered to. Many voluntarily enter a 6-month discipleship program of spiritual guidance, nutrition therapy and Bible study.

Our Father's House. Our Father's House is a discipleship program located in a rural setting in Lancaster County, Pennsylvania, which enables addicts to take the last steps on the road to a useful Christian life.

Paradise Lake Retreat Center. During the spring, fall and winter months, our children's camp at Bushkill, Pennsylvania, becomes a lovely retreat for religious gatherings of up to 200. Excellent accommodations include an on-site chapel, heated cabins, large meeting areas, recreational facilities, and delicious country-style meals. Write to: Paradise Lake Retreat Center, Box 252, Bushkill, PA 18234, or call: (717) 588-6067.

Christian Herald Magazine is contemporary—a dynamic publication that addresses the vital concerns of today's Christian. Each issue contains a sharing of true personal stories written by people who have found in Christ the strength to make a difference in the world around them.

Family Bookshelf provides a wide selection of wholesome, inspirational reading and Christian literature written by best-selling authors. All books are recommended by an Advisory Board of distinguished writers and editors.

* * *

Christian Herald ministries, founded in 1878, are supported by the voluntary contributions of individuals and by legacies and bequests. Contributions are tax deductible. Checks should be made out to: Christian Herald Children, Bowery Mission, or Christian Herald Association.

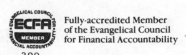

ECFA Fully-accredited Member of the Evangelical Council for Financial Accountability

389

Administrative Office:
40 Overlook Drive
Chappaqua, New York 10514
Telephone: (914) 769-9000